This book is dedicated to the immigrant spirit
and courage of my parents Marina Gonzales
Mesa and Lawerence Escobedo Mesa

—*Amalia Mesa-Bains*

In memoriam—
Gloria Anzaldúa and Octavia Butler

—*bell hooks*

bell hooks and amalia mesa-bains

homegrown
engaged cultural criticism

Cover design by Design Action.
Cover image courtesy of ImageState/Alamy.
Page design and production by Joey Fox and
the South End Press Collective.
This book was designed using Adobe InDesign CS2.

Library of Congress Cataloging-in-Publication Data
Hooks, Bell.
Homegrown : engaged cultural criticism / Bell Hooks and Amalia Mesa-Bains. -- 1st ed.
p. cm.
ISBN 0-89608-759-X
1. African Americans--Social conditions.
2. Hispanic Americans--Social conditions.
3. Mexican Americans--Social conditions.
4. Feminist criticism--United States. 5. Hooks, Bell.
6. Mesa-Bains, Amalia. 7. Ethnicity--United States.
8. Multiculturalism--United States. 9. United States--Race relations.
10. United States--Social conditions. I. Mesa-Bains, Amalia. II. Title.

E185.86.H736 2006
305.48'800973--dc22
2006013633

Printed with union leader in Canada on acid-free, recycled paper.
10 09 08 07 06   1 2 3 4 5

homegrown: Engaged Cultural Criticism
ISBN 0-89608-759-X (pbk.: alk. paper)

South End Press
7 Brookline Street, #1
Cambridge, MA 02139
http://www.southendpress.org
southend@southendpress.org
Read. Write. Revolt.

Table of Contents

Preface

"What might black women say to Chicana women? We grieve with you and we want ceremonies of reconciliation that link our goddesses and gods to each other, patterning new codices of forgiveness and triumph, sisters of the cornsilk and sisters of [the] yam....We petition the basketweavers to dream a new pattern of our knowing and loving that binds the permanent impermanence of our footprints in the sand."

—M. Jacqui Alexander, *Pedogogies of Crossing*

bell: *Homegrown: Engaged Cultural Criticism* is the culmination of an informal collaboration that began almost ten years ago, a time when there was tremendous excitement about questioning Western domination, Western hegemony, and the biases in education. Amalia, when you and I met, the areas you and I work in—cultural criticism, art marking, creative writing, teaching—were undergoing tremendous growth and transformation, largely due to the interventions and work of people of color. And you and I shared the sense that we were moving forward in antiracist, pro-woman struggles. It seemed that the movements we were invested in were responding to pressures to be less white, less racist, and less sexist.

What has become much more difficult since we met in the 1990s is that much of the movement's work and energy has been undermined by the growing state fascism and the complacency of people who benefited from movements for radical change. We have entered a period of grave silence, censorship, and violence.

Amalia: I agree. In some of my young students, I see a deeper sense of hopelessness, and for good reason—we are living in desperate times. But I think the conversation you and I have kept up over the years is very promising. We are refusing to be silenced or pitted against each other, and so are many others who are working for peace, justice, compassion.

bell: I agree. You know, we called the book *Homegrown*, because you know how homegrown food is really better for you? This conversation should nurture others. Part of why we are doing and want to publish our conversation, rather than our essays, is to speak to people who aren't necessarily essay readers, and who aren't necessarily in academic institutions, but who are, or have the potential to be "organic intellectuals," people who critically think and engage in dialectical exchange wherever they are.

Amalia: The term "homegrown" is also relevant to both of our upbringings. When I think about the *platicas*, or the little discussions, there have always been models of this kind of exchange in the Latino community, from ordinary story-telling to *corridos*, which are these running, historical songs. So, if you like, in some way we found ourselves in this homegrown model because it had resonance for each of us, as we hope it will for the folks we are hoping to reach.

bell: And by actions like these, which are forms of activism, we repudiate the notion that as cultural workers and intellectuals, we are at odds with the world that we come from. And I agree with you—in this project, we're thinking about solidarity and the links between Black culture and Latino culture. Certainly the mainstream discourse about Black-Latino relationships is very negative. We're always hearing that we have nothing in common.

Amalia: We're at a point where many of these so-called differences are constructed, precisely because there are systems that benefit from our lack of solidarity around labor, immigration, education and cultural rights, and they set in place the terminology and technology of division long ago. For instance, if you use the term Hispanic, your Spanish upbringing is privileged and your African and Indian are neutralized. All of these connections are unacknowledged, and their absence keeps us from seeing our similarities, and foregrounds our differences.

bell: I don't even think the mass media is interested in our differences as they pertain to the specificity of our cultural locations. They want all people of color to be defined in relationship to whiteness. For this reason, attention is always paid to political splits between people of color. It's also simply true that African Americans have not taken strong stands in support of bilingual education, and many conservative African Americans buy into anti-immigration racism.

Amalia: And in cities like Los Angeles, enormous political complexities are reduced to coverage suggesting that Blacks support a white candidate who may not even be progressive because he would defeat a Mexican or Chicano candidate who might privilege other Chicanos and exclude Blacks. That's all we hear. This is happening in lots of places where historically we have lived side by side, done similar jobs, and have intermarried. This is happening in places where there are deep and rooted communities, intertwined and interdependent.

bell: That's precisely why this conversation is itself a form of activism; it's our resistance to that the idea of separation. We do have differences, but our commonalities are just as strong, and they represent hope for resistance and freedom. Homegrown is an expression, it's a declaration and a bearing witness of that solidarity. It is a denial of the notion, the false assumption that we are not connected.

Amalia: We are connected.

FAMILY

bell: My earliest childhood experiences were shaped by fundamentalist Christian beliefs. As much as anything else, they framed what girls could or could not do. For instance, on Sunday girls couldn't wear pants, we couldn't play music, and we couldn't walk across the pulpit. The pulpit was considered a sacred space that a female—of any age—could not walk across, because she would defile it. In church between Sunday school and the morning service, I'd see all these boys running around and crossing the pulpit, but girls were always stopped. It was an early indoctrination into sexist thinking.

Amalia: My family life was totally shaped by Catholicism—a hybrid of Mexican and US Catholicism, as it included Irish priests from Ireland. There was this strange kind of mix of oratory and liturgy and beauty, but it was certainly fundamentalist. Catholicism belonged to the altar boys. There are altar girls now, but not then. So the fact that women maintained home altars or yard shrines posed alternatives to the conventional norm.

bell: Whereas my mother's churchgoing was very tied with her class mobility. In fact, she wanted to get away from the Pentecostal tent meetings that working-class and poor people often attended. She wanted us to belong to a church that was modern, and for her this meant sedate, and no shouting and jumping for joy. The church only had power, but not all of it.

Amalia: Was it still Baptist?

bell: Yes, all the Black churches were Baptist, but Mama still wanted to rise in her class position, and this meant involvement in a church where there wasn't a lot of shouting or emotional release. In our church there was one day, Communion Sunday on the first of the month, when people could give testimony and sing in the old ways. Elderly folk in the church continued to shout, but shouting was something that my mother's generation had begun to see as unseemly.

Amalia: My mother also played a pivotal role in my Catholic upbringing. Partly because her mother took her to a Catholic convent school and enrolled her as a student, and she didn't come back for her. The school took her in as an orphan. As a result, my mother had a very intense devotional relationship to the church, yet by the time we were born, she and my father were practicing birth control. For people of their generation and background, this was almost unheard of. And we were really different because there was only my brother and I. All of our other family members, and relatives, had five and sometimes even ten kids.

bell: Like my family—six girls and one boy! Where did you grow up?

Amalia: This was in Santa Clara, California. My dad came when he was a little boy, during the Mexican Revolution, around 1917. There were work furlough programs then, and Mexicans were going to Denver and to Pueblo, Colorado to work. My mother came across with her mom on a day pass in the 1920s to do domestic work on the American side. Both of them ended up staying here. They didn't have papers for many years, but later they finally got them. However, this meant that for many years they lived in a very isolated way, as many undocumented people do—they were always careful to stay to themselves and not break rules. As a result, their community was tightly circumscribed, except for the church. But once my mother started practicing birth control, she couldn't attend services anymore. So attending church became my responsibility. I was the little emissary, I would attend church and I would come back and report. I would tell everything that happened. I would save the little brochures, the church newsletter, and I would cut out the pictures in the little church newsletters of the religious images. And they were, you know, really famous religious paintings. Those were my first images of art, really.

bell: I've written about this. For many African American working-class people, the first art we encounter is religious iconography. In my childhood, I saw were the cheap reproductions of Leonardo, and Michelangelo…

Amalia: Caravaggio…

bell: …all of that. But I was not born into an atmosphere where art was discussed. Neither my grandparents nor my parents talked about art or the imagery we saw, which in fact was the juxtaposition of family photographs and religious iconography—prints of, you know, religious scenes.

Amalia: We had "holy cards," and sometimes little books which depicted the lives of the saints. For me, the lives of the saints were like soap operas. They were fantastical! Lucy was blinded, with her eyes on the little plate that she carried. San Sebastian was shot through with arrows. They were really very graphic, physical, and even sexual. I think that's why everyone loved their stories. And I always thought that the saints were like this big extended family, and through them, we seemed to be related to God, Jesus, to Mary, and all these intriguing people. These images were also part of that relationship to religion, not spirituality.

bell: That's how I came to art, thinking about religious and family images, and then getting into the public school. I attended our little all-Black school, where art classes were offered. The good fortune of that time was that everyone took art classes. In those days, studying art was okay.

Amalia: Did you feel that you had an aptitude from the beginning, that you could draw well? Did you like to copy pictures? How did you know art was a cultural practice for you?

bell: I couldn't draw well at all. I wanted to draw well and I took classes, worked really hard, but I didn't have an innate gift. Among working-class Black folks, if you could draw well people encouraged you.

Amalia: That's why I was asking about your aptitude, because that's what some of my relatives picked up on. I'm in the third generation of artists in my family, on my father's side. There are my great-uncles, my uncles, and in my generation there's like five or six of us. In the generation after us, there's even more. And I had an aptitude, I had a gift. People saw it right away, and encouraged me. My father had a brother and an uncle who were talented and made things, so he knew that I would become an artist. That's why they supported my work, even though they didn't think it would be a job or a way of life.

bell: My father had an elderly first cousin in Chicago, who painted dark, oil portraits of nude women. He was the first artist I knew, my cousin Schuyler—even his name was exotic. And in my teens, my parents let me go to Chicago and I saw his work. I was shocked, because it was all nudes!

Amalia: What did other people say in the family?

bell: They saw his art practice as weird. They thought the fact that he painted and saw himself as an artist was a cover for laziness. He wore a beret, and spent time alone in a basement studio dreaming and making art.

Amalia: He was a bohemian.

bell: Totally. He affirmed my interest in art, even though I did not draw well. Schuyler encouraged this passion, and so did my high school art teacher, Mr. Harrell. I've written a lot about my high school art teacher, because he really encouraged me. He saw me as a potential artist, and he displayed my work and awarded me prizes. My parents were opposed to this interest, because there was no money for luxuries. When I painted, I could only paint during school hours, using the school's resources. And when I wanted to enter one of my paintings into one of the art shows, I had to have work framed to enter. My parents said, "Sorry, you can't do this, we're not made of money and we don't think there's a need for this." I had painted this very primitive portrait of a little boy. And my parents couldn't understand it as art. It wasn't…

Amalia: Representational enough?

bell: The world of abstract art was just weird to them. But my art teacher helped me to gather scraps of wood, and we created a primitive frame so that my work could be in the show. I remember my picture hanging in the show, and my parents were proud of the fact that I'd won third place, but this did not mean they supported my desire to make art.

Amalia: Since making art was part of my family, they were willing to commit whatever they could afford. When I was very young, maybe seven or eight, there was a back porch on our house where the dog stayed and there was a washing machine, the kind you cranked by hand. They set up a little easel there. By then my father was no longer working in the cannery—he might have been in the grocery business. So he knew people at the store, and he would go to the meat market and get rolls of butcher paper. When he got come, he'd put rocks on the paper to flatten it out, and that became my art paper. When I went to high school, they bought me a painting set. Because it was very expensive, it was a big deal. Even then, I saw art is a kind of doorway one enters, which can lead to freedom. Sometimes people try to keep the door shut and you have to bang to get in. Sometimes people shove you through the door because they're so sure you should go there.

Unfortunately, in high school I didn't get along with my art teachers, because they wanted me to make work in a certain kind of way. I didn't want to do it. I vividly remember one of my teachers marking up my image to show me how to do it correctly.

I tore it up and left the class. Of course I was sent to the office for being rude to the teacher, and I kept saying, "But he was rude to me, he marked on my drawing." No one thought I had that kind of authorship yet, so it was not mine.

bell: By comparison, my high school art teacher was an Italian immigrant. He understood what it meant to be an outsider.

Amalia: A white teacher in an all-Black school?

bell: I went to all-Black schools until I was in the ninth grade. When I went to racially integrated schools and went to art classes, there were easels. Most of the white teachers were racist, but our high school art teacher was a cosmopolitan man. He wore black, that's one of the things I remember. Looking back I see now that he, like my cousin Schuyler, was almost like a caricature of an artist. But since he was the most cosmopolitan person I had ever encountered in my life, I associated all of that with art—freedom, independence of mind and being.

Art class was the one place in high school where I felt liberated from the drive to be the perfect Black student, always smart and uplifting my race. In art class, I could be whatever I wanted to be. He stressed that we could be whatever we wanted to be. One of his assignments was to have each of us choose an artist, study them, and try to paint in their tradition. In class, I learned about William deKooning, and I chose to pattern my work after his. Later I learned that other Black people have had that relationship with deKooning's work, and I've tried to think about why that is the case, was it the colors that he chose, he used so many dark hues.

Amalia: Or that fact that he, like many modernists, quasi-contemporaries, really studied African art, and art from other parts of the world and really integrated them, and those gestures could be seen in their painting.

bell: Absolutely, but despite his support and interventions, my art teacher was seen as somewhat suspect. He was not a Southerner, and that set him even further apart from the other teachers. In high school, I really wanted to join this new world, and my parents told me, "Absolutely not. How will you make any money?"

Amalia: By the time I left home to go to college, my parents knew I would be an artist, but they didn't want me to suffer, so we made a compromise. I agreed that I would study commercial art, which was very "en vogue" in the early sixties. Then when no one was looking, I switched to painting. I don't think they realized it till I graduated. It didn't really prepare me for any kind of living, at least in that era. It did open up this whole wide world of people who were different.

bell: Where was this, Amalia?

Amalia: San Jose State University. I went first to a junior college for a couple of years, but then I went to San Jose State. It was very wild and bohemian and there were no Mexicans, except for maybe me. At that time, 20,000 students were enrolled there, and the school had a big Greek system, with a lot of fraternities and sororities that were very, very white.

bell: Before I attended Stanford, I went to a white women's college in the Midwest. There some of the depression I felt in my high school years, the suicidal depression set in. It was about being an outsider, and knowing I didn't fit in there. But my parents were pleased with this college because there were a lot of rules.

Amalia: They liked the social controls.

bell: And I'd won a general scholarship. They could drive me there. It was a kind of finishing school in some ways. You didn't have to take art classes, but if you showed an interest you could have an easel and you could paint. So I always had my own easel, and I would go to the studio to paint. Yet throughout college, all the people in that world were white men. It was the same at this women's college. Art remained a white, hegemonic world. So I began to get into theatre, too. You've said that artistic endeavors—whether theatre, visual arts, or creative writing—offered space for people of color to be ourselves. In so many ways, those spaces attracted the white folk who were outsiders and who didn't belong.

Amalia: As you've been talking, I've been thinking how I didn't fit in with the Mexicans, either! First off, I'm from a small family, and already, people are wondering. Then, my first name is Maxine—Amalia is my middle name. Maxine? What kind of a name is that? It's not a Mexican name. Is it the Andrews sisters? Is it Maxmilian Carlotta? What is it?

bell: What was your mother thinking, Amalia?

Amalia: She said it reminded her of a movie star's name: "Maxine Mesa." And in the 1930s and 1940s—I was born in 1943—Mexicans saw boxing and movie stardom as the way out. For Mexican girls like me, I called it the "Delores Del Río phenomenon." Years later, these images and entities are paramount in my own artwork, because they came from my mother, giving me ideas about what I would be. So "Maxine Mesa" was supposed to be a movie star.

Then, another mark against me—they didn't pierce my ears. They didn't want any piercing. I've never met a Mexican in my childhood that did not have pierced ears, except me.

bell: And wait, what was that about?

Amalia: I don't know. No one's ever told me. And so I had them pierced when I was eighteen.

bell: My mother and father were very opposed to piercing. We all longed to be pierced.

Amalia: Well, the first earrings Mexican girls wear are little baby crosses, as infants. In retrospect, it was very clear that somebody had already decided that I wasn't going to be like the rest of the Mexicans. And as I got older, I feel like I located myself in a space in which I was not "Mexican," but I could never be "white." I know the language for it now: the *interestus*, or the space in between two spaces. So all of the peers that I ran around with in high school were the very popular white girls. But on the weekends and at home, my friends were Mexican kids who were related indirectly to my family through *compradasto*, or godparentage. They were the children that my parents helped to baptize, and they all knew me.

bell: Because I was seen as different and strange at home, I was being emotionally abused and at times whipped.

Amalia: And did your parents do that because they were afraid that if you didn't learn to behave, things would be worse for you?

bell: Absolutely. So the only way that I could escape censure was to be talented and win their approval for something. So I became very active in acting and debate and won lots of prizes. I painted, I did theatre, I was on the debating team, and I was "booksmart" as well. And because of my mother's class aspirations—she didn't want to be a backwoods person like her mother—I took piano and organ lessons. I was going to be a gifted, talented, person on all fronts. I would know about appropriate manners and etiquette. I feel I was part of a wave of working-class Black people integrating the educational system in the US, and our parents were determined that we would be the best at everything.

Amalia: It's almost like the talented tenth in a way.

bell: Something like that. The idea of "racial uplift" was certainly part of what propelled me and my neighborhood friends forward. So I always think it's funny when folks think that contemporary feminism made me who I am. I became who I am because of my own refusal to accept patriarchy *as a girl*, and because I witnessed my mother's resistance.

It's ironic—on one hand, my mother didn't finish high school, bore six daughters, and she dealt with many "unchosen" pregnancies, which I think are quite different from "unwanted" pregnancies. Like many women of the 1950s, she came to terms with these unchosen pregnancies and all her children became desired children. Yet she raised her girls to focus on not getting pregnant before marriage, and on getting our education. My dad said to her—and to us—that too much education made women undesirable. His message was "you're not going to have a husband" and "you're going to be too willful." Indeed, a lot of the beatings my dad gave me were to break my will. When I realized that I was going to have to resist this domination in every form, my feminist resistance began.

Contrary to the assumption that feminism and Blackness do not fit, my resistance to gender began in the heart of Black experience, in the heart of patriarchy. Even so, many people want to see the Black experience as not being patriarchal. They have gotten carried away with the focus on households headed by single women, and they can't acknowledge that these families can be just as patriarchal as two-parent households! They also erase the fact that in the traditional Black community, when Black people were citizens of the "new world" before enslavement, and after slavery, there were few homes without an adult male authority figure. He might be an uncle, a brother, a grandparent, a friend, or a lover, but the idea that there are all these homes with no men present, there were all these women-headed empires is a fiction, and a fiction of modernity. Of course, the formation of state-controlled public housing projects created communities where adult male presence was not welcomed.

Amalia: Welfare laws prevented men from being there legally.

bell: Exactly. The state gave women housing but threatened to take it away if there was an adult male present! This is an example of the white male supremacist patriarchal state exiling Black men. Prior to public housing for female-headed households, there were always adult males present who acted as authority figures. Growing up in a Christian patriarchal context I realized quite early as a girl that I was going to have to define myself in resistance to patriarchy. Importantly, feminism did not come into being simply because people invented the word "feminism." Social movements against injustice emerge long before they're named. Whenever women resisted patriarchy, feminism existed, long before women got together and organized around this particular word.

Amalia: I think about it in the same way. Women may not have articulated their goals for creating equity for themselves in the same way before the movement, but there were always feminist actions and there were always feminists.

For example, look at Emma Tenayuca, who was in her twenties when she led a strike of Mexican American pecan shellers in San Antonio, Texas in 1936—the Workers Alliance strike became a key event in the political liberation of Mexican Americans in San Antonio. And Luisa Moreno and Josefina Fierro de Bright were leaders in the United Cannery, Agricultural Packing and Allied Workers (UCAPAWA) in Los Angeles in 1940. They both addressed the Spanish Speaking People's Congress and worked with garment workers. (Moreno was from a fairly wealthy family in Guatemala, but came to the US at a young age.) Each of these women made enormous contributions, only to be deported during the Mexican repatriation movement. In fact, approximately 500,000 Mexican Americans—more than half with US citizenship—were sent back to Mexico, or hounded to death during the McCarthy era because they worked for collective goals or represented "Communism."

As a Chicana, I have always seen these women in a genealogy of feminism which holds relevance for me. And as a young woman, I really didn't have a relationship with white feminism. I graduated from college in 1966, so by the late 1960s I was engaged with the Chicano movement, which for me, preceded feminism. During the 1970s, I experienced the empowerment of women and watched who assumed control of certain elements of the movement, even though women's issues and patriarchy were often sub-sumed under the banner of unity.

I've written about this "domestic tension" between daughters and our moms, our grandmothers, our godmothers, or our *tías*. They created worlds within worlds—spaces dedicated to women within the household. My childhood kitchen was like that. My mother, my tía, my grandmother, my godmother and my cousins created a world where they would talk about men, or talk about what they needed to do for us as children. They seemed to have an alliance with each other, and to know that they were at odds, at times, with the men in our family. So while there was a sense of resistance, it was never direct.

That community created a sense of belonging that I de-sired, but I knew I would have to break with it. Because it was always expected that as women we would have to silently resist, and I didn't want to silently resist! So I reached a point where I couldn't emulate the very women who had loved me, had raised me, and had given me a sense of who I was.

bell: This separation plays out in many ways. When I im-mersed myself in intellectual work, there was a tension between that and my embrace of traditional "feminine" concerns—I was into clothes and into being "beautiful," as well as being smart. I felt I could be this total, sexy, feminine female and still be re-spected for my intelligence. At eighteen and nineteen, I did not know that looking feminine, trying to be glamorous, made one suspect in the academic world. The white women who were within the educational structures weren't trying to be gorgeous or sexy.

Amalia: I know exactly what you're talking about, and some people have even asked me if I didn't see a contradiction between my fairly feminine dress and my concerns with beauty and my activism around feminism and class issues. I've always said that within the culture there is a real regard given to beauty. If you come from poor villages in Mexico or your family is from there, you can see it in the way people stack fruit in front of their stalls, or the way they hang colored plastic bags. They take advantage of every opportunity to create beauty—each thing has its place, and it's been thoughtfully decided. It's not accidental—it's really very conscious. Growing up with this heritage, there wasn't any other way I could have seen myself. As an artist, I extend my aesthetics into every choice I make about my life—the food I eat, the plate that the food is on, the clothes I put on my body. So I know what you're talking about. There is a point where our desire to be activists and advocates may clash with the clothes we're wearing or even the cars we may drive. At some point, questions may be asked. That's why tension is such an important word to me—sometimes I don't feel that the contradictions can truly be resolved.

bell: For Black women, the contradictions about our relationship to beauty are rooted in the slave experience and our life in white supremacist culture. Slaves were not working in the homes of poor white people; they were working in the homes of the white wealthy. And if you visit any of these surviving plantations today, you find that the women in these settings, especially white ruling-class women, were concerned with aesthetics. They were trying to get the best antiques and things that were popular at that time, whether it was a silver tea set or a particular kind of linen and embroidery.

The taste of people like both of my great-grandmothers and my mother's mother was certainly shaped by their exposure from working in these homes. My obsession with textiles and fibers was cultivated in childhood by Sarah Oldham, my maternal grandmother. She was a consummate quilt maker, a person who was highly conscious of differences in cottons and silks. This attention to detail may have come from her experience of being a caretaker and creator of domestic culture, and of the beauty within that culture. Because we all know that if the silver was polished, it was not polished by Miss Ann! It was polished by the servant, and she developed a body of knowledge about objects, aesthetic objects.

Consequently, my grandmother—a woman who didn't read or write—wanted me to understand the differences between an eighteenth-century and a nineteenth-century antique, and to comprehend all these things she had picked up from working for the white ruling classes.

Amalia: As I listen to you, I've been thinking about my own mother. She worked for a fairly wealthy family in southern California, and took care of their young son. She really saw after him, probably much more than his own parents. But she got her first job with this family as their maid. She was around fourteen and went to an employment agency. They asked if she had ever cleaned houses—she said yes she knew how to clean and she was very good at it. So the woman was having a party that night, and they sent her right out. So the woman liked my mother. And on the second or third day she was there, my mother cleaned an antique chair, thinking it was dirty because it had stains and marks around the grooves. She furiously assaulted it with all kinds of cleaning potions, and when the woman found her she had practically taken the paint off.

For her, these were the early days of life in that world, and until I was much older, I didn't realize that growing up with table settings and cloth napkins was not the norm for most working-class people! My aesthetic voice sprung from a home in which my mother had spent her formative years living among wealthy people and handling extremely expensive items. It also came from the church. That is another area where my aesthetic dispositions were highly developed.

bell: Another important part of this sort of relationship to beauty was the relationship to color and nature. My grandmother was a great gardener—the front of the house was given over to flowers, and then the back of her house was given over to the garden. There was such a whole sense of color in nature. The tomatoes were so beautifully red; the delphiniums were so outstandingly blue. There is a wonderful passage in Toni Morrison's *The Bluest Eye* where she is talking about the South and contrasting it to the industrialized North. She described the South as this place of color where one sees and experiences everything more vividly; there is a lushness to color. That world of natural beauty in the South has shaped the construction of my aesthetics. Picking the grapes from our vines and my grandmother making wine, the dusky purple of the grapes, and the color of the wine. I can remember us all gushing over the color—the color of the peppers that she grew, strung together, and hung. This is where I gained a sense of nature as the place where one is grounded and renewed spiritually, and where I learned to value the environment, and understand that I was defined—in part—by my relationship to the earth.

By contrast, Rosa Bell, my mama, represented the tyranny of modernity—her approach was to get rid of nature. "Put up some curtains so you can't see the trees." "Get rid of everything in order to have this new and modern life." "Get rid of antique furniture, get rid of quilts, everything is about the new." "Put plastic on your new sofa." My mother's aesthetic was shaped by women's magazines which pushed an orthodoxy of what women should wear and buy. There was tension and conflict between the world that my grandmother ushered us into and the world that my mother wanted to create. One world was about ancestors, memory, and the past; the latter was about the present, the new, and the disposable. In that world, forgetting became a rite of passage.

Amalia: This is such a tremendous loss, because these are the things that hold us together over time, because that piecing together is almost like making a memory. I was growing up in the 1950s—when your mother is reading these magazines—and I'm trying to figure out how to be a white American teenager when I am not. One of the salvations for me was that my mother could sew. I always struggled with my weight as a child—I was not really heavy, but I was not a thin child, and even then that was beginning to be the preference. And my mother was able to interpret fashion and make it for me out of materials she would collect, so when the other girls were wearing these little Chesterfield coats, I had a "cookie coat" based on a Dior image my mother had seen, and she fashioned it together out of several different patterns. It was very large and oversized, and it had hand-rolled edges on the cuffs and collar, and it had a center seam and the front of it was notched, and the only thing that held it together was these two giant buttons that were the size of very large cookies, and so my friends dubbed it the "Cookie coat."

In some way my mother had the courage to sense that I could be different, and she would help me be different. I always thought it was because we didn't have enough money for me to buy the clothes that other kids had, but sewing may have been her own way to express and experience fashion, style, and beauty. I was just the beneficiary of her work.

bell: It was just the opposite for my mother. She had less power in her house than her mother did—my grandmother was an empress of domesticity, of creativity. In the agrarian world, the central thing is the growing and production of food. My grandmother's power flowed from the things she could grow. My mother turned her back on that and sensed that my dad represented a new generation. As a result, she had much less power than her own mother.

My father was a Black infantryman who went to World War II. He was one of that first group of poor Black men, of working-class Black men, who traveled the world. They went to Paris and London and Germany. This marked the beginning of many Black people's relationship to the home, because the men who come back from this war will be in charge. Daddy did not want our mother to work. He wanted her to be a lady, Susie Homemaker, an imitation of white womanhood.

The fifties were a turning point. Up until then, I think most Black women, especially working-class and poor Black women, were not trying to imitate white womanhood. The Black women of my grandmother's generation had contempt for white females, seeing them as kind of fragile and useless. Because those Black women were the domestic goddesses in white homes—they were the ones that made things happen—they saw those white women as dolls, as less than real. And out of that came the saying that was passed down by the Black women, my aunt, great-aunt, people who worked as maids, "I've never met a white female over the age of twelve that I can respect."

Amalia: My mother told me very peculiar things about white people when we were young. If I went to a white person's house she would say to me, "Now first of all don't ask them for beans. They won't have any tortillas. Remember what I told you about the silverware. And don't say anything if the house smells funny to you." She always thought that the white house would smell funny to us, and I think she meant that it wouldn't have the smell of familiar foods, it would have a different smell. And she would also assume that certain things would be done for me, which never were, because these were often middle-class white people where I would go to visit. And these observations came out of her relationships with people whose lives she knew intimately, because she took care of everything for them.

bell: You just brought up such a crucial thing regarding the aesthetics of poor, disenfranchised people of color. Historically, we've equated whiteness with beauty. Today many people of color have a kind of fantasy about whiteness. When I first left home for Stanford, I must admit I shared this fantasy. But I was a world away from the South, and I would go to these wealthy white people's homes, or upper-class homes, and they would be dirty. It was such a contrast between the ideas of whiteness that my mom—who was so influenced by magazines and culture—had conjured up, and the reality, again. Like your mom, my mother worked as a maid for well-off white people who were conscious of their status. She had no conception of a kind of funky white culture of privilege where everything would be dirty and smelly and no one cared. Initially, one of the reservations I had about the mainstream feminist movement was its complete disdain of beauty.

Amalia: These ideas are still very dominant in the art world, and not only held by feminists. Any artist who seeks to make work with elements focused on beauty, instead of irony or parody, is suspect.

bell: And who would ever have thought that there would be a tension or conflict between being a thinking artist and be-ing engaged in the practice of making beauty. Even when I was nineteen years old, writing my first feminist book and obsessed with feminism, people would come to my home and be astonished that I was also obsessed with the beauty in my home environment. I was one of those young folk without money who always believed that I could have beautiful things. Poverty or not, I will have my cashmere coat, it would just be a vintage cashmere coat that I ruthlessly, relentlessly hunted down at the flea market. And of course, I couldn't have been at a better historical moment—back then, in the sixties, the flea market stuff was the rage!

Amalia: Black culture has contributed enormously to fashion and style in this country. In the past our aesthetic was informed by a sense of innovation and defiance of the norm. Street style was something that others eventually copied, so then you disposed of it—if they figured out how to do it, you don't want to be doing it.

I thought about this the other day as I was looking at the images of the caste paintings in Mexico, called the *castas* paintings. Fifty-three racial categories were depicted. It looked like the world of apartheid, where you would determine which race was mixed together, so they were the combination of African, Indian, and European. And as there were rules that went with the codes of dress, so the castas paintings will show a man, woman, and child. But every once in a while there is the castas painting that will show two women. In one of the most famous ones is a white Spanish woman and an African woman standing side by side in almost identical dress except that African-descended women in Mexico at that time, this was under Spanish Colonial rule, were forbidden to wear certain elements that would in a way imitate the ruling class. They weren't supposed to wear lace and they weren't supposed to wear gold jewelry, and later, when the little pocket watches came in, they weren't supposed to wear those. There are stories of *pulata* women who are wearing yards and yards of lace, and they have six or seven watches sewn onto their skirts. So they are constantly, even in this period of violence and brutality, defying one's skin through the subverting the norms of dress and style.

bell: And I think about it now when I see kids on the street and I realize that innovation, that defiance, that capacity to bridge a divide—because style in African American life has been kind of revolutionary fashion statement—is now in peril. But I often grapple with the difference between style and aesthetics, because I think that many young African American people are interested in style, particularly in relation to clothing or music, but they are not interested in a holistic aesthetic, particularly in relationship to one's environment. I see myself as a person who is both obsessed with style—I say my tombstone will read, "I died for style"—but style is only one component of my aesthetic.

Amalia: I wish that in the process of consuming style there might be a consumption of an aesthetic disposition, but they don't seem to go together. And part of it is the enormous influence media has on consumption. There is this constant pressure on people to consume, but nowhere in that process are we really free to make aesthetic decisions—what are really being marketed to us are products that will lead us to another product that will lead us to another product.

bell: Exactly. So the idea of the innovation, the notion that you might take the product and totally alter it for your own, again, sensibility, I think is increasingly dying out. In my work, that is what I've called oppositional consciousness. That instead of giving in to the cultural domination you in a sense outwit the cultural domination by saying, "We continue with the project of our own humanization in the face of colonization, in the face of a world that wishes to colonize our minds." That's why there was a distinct difference between the sense of power, of woman power, and the power against whiteness at my grandmother's house, and our own house, which was the epitome of the encroachment of a kind of patriarchal dominance and embraced a colonizing white aesthetic.

Amalia: When Tommy Hilfiger walked in and took over that realm of hip-hop clothing, then innovation was over. If a white man can figure out how to do this, you know, forget all the other Sean "Puffy" Combs or any of the rest that will come along. Now, it's already been done. It's already been consumed and appropriated and then resold. Before, the first thing to happen was the emergence of a very distinct street style. Then, designers would observe it and translate it, but they would never try to sell it back to the street.

bell: The resistance of the street was, "How dare you try to sell back to me this appropriation." The street defies that by immediately creating anew. But now people don't want to cut off the label, or any part of the connection to Hilfiger or Versace. This erasure of creativity, this recolonization of imagination, creates mannequins. Everything becomes part of a new plantation economy, so the Black body becomes the mannequin on which white fantasies of otherness are played out.

Amalia: And it's an extension too of the marketing of identity, of the cashing in on the original struggles that have influenced us so powerfully: the feminist movement, the Chicana movement, Black Power. These were real and engaged struggles, sometimes violent, very often dangerous, not always understood by the generation before us. But they were real moments of struggle that begat certain directions and attitudes that people took, and there was a certain affectation of style even then, but the struggle for one's own aesthetics was more dominant than the style. What you have now then is the marketing of racialized identities as tools for consumption. And certain racialized bodies and images are associated with hipness, coolness, edginess. So all kinds of youth all over the world are appropriating that style as a way of, sort of, countering authority, stating their rebelliousness, and wanting to be seen as significant. So that when you have an Eminem, for example, someone who takes on the manifestation of Blackness and style and the language and body but can still engage in homophobic and misogynistic language.

bell: And racist language, then you know it is only a style and it is not anchored in any way with any critical knowledge of what it means to be Black. Or, by extension, they are so uncreative as to be easily adaptable. For example, we can now say well, here's this white boy who plays the blues, and it's the same blues. You strip the blues of its complex psychohistory, and listeners forget that it's not just this thing that's about can you play an instrument and can you sing a certain style, but that it brings with it an ethos of culture and experience. You strip it of the ethos that gives it its particularity, and say well, you see, it was not that unique or great. Because if it were, it would not be so easily translatable or appropriated.

Amalia: There were legions of women with no involvement in the struggle for social rights within the Mexican community, but they had this great affection and affinity for altars and various forms of imagery. They thought these were things they could take. And the battles over appropriation became very heated—people would throw the word "essentialist" at you. "Do you think you just own this culture? What do you mean?" And then I remember many of us saying, "No we don't own it, but we earned it—it's ours."

One of the biggest struggles Latinos in the US face is that we produce aesthetic materials that are relocated within a tourist industry. People looking for their "border fix" might buy a serape, get some dirt from Chimayo, or have chimichangas. The look, the food, the land, the clothes and the music all get rolled up into one.

Also, I think, in the majority Latinos are associated with a "mañana mentality," or the tomorrow time. In other words, the dominant culture sees us as lazy, unfocused, and never in a hurry. But if you look underneath, what you find is a culture where the word *encantada* means enchanted—I give over myself to you, you've cast a spell on me, and time does not limit what we can accomplish. Time is to be expanded and used, because the longer I can be with you, the deeper is my relationship to you. I am not in a hurry to leave you.

I am so intrigued about this time thing, and I've read your writing on prisons, so I've been thinking about what Chicanas do in prison: they tattoo, they do envelope art, they find various and sundry ways to do something with their hands. *Pino* art, pinos are the handkerchief art. They get ballpoint pens when they can, and draw on the handkerchiefs that they wear. So even when people are relegated to prison, where the time is endless, they find some way to reinvent beauty.

bell: This is one reason that capitalism has entered prisons and turned them into factories. The managers and the politicians are determined to prevent incredible revolutionary spirits—like Malcolm X—from flourishing there, so in comes the mind-numbing factory, as well as the creation of a contemporary slave system which requires people to work all day for very, very low wages.

This is an incredible assault on the sensibilities of young people, who make up a large proportion of the prison population. As someone fortunate enough to be "free," I am able to nurture my imagination, and devote myself to expressing and encountering it. In my life, I've travelled all over the world to see beautiful art. But my pilgrimage to the Shrine of the Black Madonna in Montserrat nourished my soul. This image of a beautiful, dark Madonna, blessing and healing the world, is counterhegemonic: it challenges the equation of Blackness with ugliness.

Amalia: I've travelled to Montserrat, too. And I remember going up a tiny staircase with people in directly front of you, and people directly behind you. I only had a moment to go through the little room where she was. There was Plexiglass over most of it, with only her hand open to your touch. As we passed by, people touched or kissed the hand. And in that moment I gave over my American fears of bacteria and germs, and I was transported. I felt like I was the only one in the room.

FEMINIST
ICONOGRAPHY

bell: The church and religion were essential to the construction of your aesthetic. As a poor and working-class girl, the first place I saw paintings, not reproductions, was in the church.

Amalia: And in Mexican Catholicism, the Virgin is almost more dominant than Christ. If I look at my aesthetics, they come from my family and from the church—both highly gendered spaces for me, spaces where images of women, the role of women, the practices of women, the spirituality of women, the domestic labor of women, have a centrality. So much so that I found a way in religion to dispense with Christ. He was never integral in any way to my belief system and he remains outside of it. For me, women's saints and women's deities were able to represent the beauty that you were talking about earlier.

bell: The root meaning of the word "ecstasy" is to stand outside of. I remember that sense of awe, particularly as a Black-skinned woman thinking of what takes place in the reimagining of the Black female not as whore, bitch, or bearer of violence, but as bearer of the sacred, the healing, and the inspiring.

Amalia: This is like Califia—the first Amazon, the Black woman in the new world, the figure of power, the leader. California is named for her! It's also similar to the representation of Kali as this triple goddess, or the elements of scarification on the face of Montserrat which make her so clearly African, even though the tour guides have made up all of these reasons why she isn't Black. They tell all kinds of stories—like it might be the smoke from the candles—because they simply cannot accept a Madonna figure that could be Black.

For a while, I explored these images in my own work. In many respects, it's what prompted me to look at curating. I had seen the appropriation of La Virgen de Guadalupe on a large scale. She is a very accessible image—she is an image that is dark-skinned, and always associated in the history of Mexico with indigenous rights and struggles against taxation and the Spanish. She is also associated with the Tonantzin, the earth mothers who came before the really old goddess figures, so she is a perfect symbol of cultural hybridity.

Some people even refer to her as an aperture. In other words, people can put their needs and their longing for protection, sustenance, and empowerment in the space where she sits. She has functioned for centuries in this way. But there came a time when it became necessary to locate her critical cultural positioning and situate this figure within a broader context of struggle and history, so that even if people consumed her in a popular sense—buying embroidered jackets, jeans, T-shirts, mugs, or earrings—it wouldn't matter. We would have definitively claimed and named her for what she really was, as this figure of power, defense, revolution and agency. People like Yolanda López and Ester Hernández have done this by creating images where she's wearing shoes, or karate fighting, or jogging.

When these figures like these enter popular culture and are consumed, we have to find ways to deepen and articulate their meanings across communities. Without this effort, they can be vandalized, culturally strip-mined, and visually overtaken by people who use want to use them, destructively.

bell: I agree. Unfortunately, African Americans have not been interested in reclaiming representations of black Madonnas. Instead, some of us have attempted to do this with the Venus

Hottentot image. However, this does not work or translate as well, because the Venus Hottentot image has never been an everyday icon. While academics and artists might be aware of her troubling legacy, it doesn't reach the majority of folks, who struggle daily with how Black women are represented.

Amalia: I think the fact that people are so familiar with her is what provokes some of the enormous controversies about images of the La Virgen de Guadalupe. She is an "everyday icon," and people really feel quite close to her and can be easily offended if others abuse her.

bell: And this is a sensitive point, because most constructions of Black femaleness are tied to representations that are hateful and ugly, so that the idea of an icon that can stand in resistance becomes further and further away.

For example, it is interesting to think of the iconic role played by Angela Davis. Perhaps her image has been tied so frequently to the misogynistic patriarchal ethos that informed the black liberation struggle that it has lost its some of its subversiveness? But many years ago it would have been considered somewhat treasonous for Spike Lee to make the documentary *Four Little Girls* and not include Angela Davis; she came to critical consciousness around racism because she was from Birmingham, and because she heard about the church bombing while she was studying in Europe. This happened in her childhood world, yet Lee completely ignored her in his otherwise powerful film. We work against that. That's the whole point of our efforts—to reenter the space of artistic representation. So little is changing, and at times it seems that the situation is actually worsening.

Amalia: Yes. As we move from generation to generation, it's never clear whether or not the women coming behind us will engage in the reclamation of key figures. I think in our generation, at least among Chicanos, there's actually quite a great activity around that, so I'm not sure for us that I would say it is worsening, but I do think it is a critical question.

bell: Mainstream visual images are certainly not radical or visionary. In the world of letters and writing, there has been an expanding sense of Black female icons that people can choose from. But most of the images coming out of the art world—including those produced by Black artists—continue the colonizer-colonized discourse of desire, which is very different than the discourse of freedom. The last twenty years have afforded us tremendous space to analyze and interrogate representations, and I strongly feel that we need to rapidly produce a new field of images of decolonized representations. I push myself to do that; creating children's picture books allows me to collaborate with illustrators to produce new and different images. Writing *Happy to Be Nappy* and talking about "our hair being like flower petals" is a new way to speak about the Black female body. Contrast that with the book *Nappy Hair,* which says, "Your hair is bad, but you can come to love it." Well, that's the same old stale colonizing, racist, sexist message. I wanted to create a totally different, joyous sense of Black girlhood.

When we talk about images, representations, my mentor is an artist like Frida Kahlo, who inspired me from the moment I discovered her work. I admired the images she produced, but I also appreciated how her self-invention. Up until that moment, only successful and recognized white male artists had dared to project their portraits as worthy of the global gaze. What Frida Kahlo did, as a woman of color, was a radical intervention. Look at the forms and strategies she chose to use to create her own image: Rembrandt painted endless self-portraits, and he did them within a canon of painting that was clearly European in its source; Frida used strategies associated with folk artists—she painted on tin, created broadsides, and borrowed from popular imagery—so she fundamentally challenged the folk art–fine art binary.

Amalia: She came from Hungarian-Jewish ancestry on her father's side, which she repressed as the years went on, and the attitudes that she had as an activist also came from her father. He took particularly strong stands around World War II because of what was happening in Nazi Germany. And she also had the open relationship to Communism that many Mexican intellectuals in from that periodshared, and she tried very hard to embrace her mother's indigenous ancestry. There was a point where her choice to suppress her European ancestry and claim her Mexicanness created issues in her relationship with Diego Rivera. She was a very complicated person, and not easily understood; she was a person who lived within contradictions, and transcended them because of her intellectual and spiritual energies.

But Frida has been pursued by white feminists in the US who have deracinated and depoliticized her. They have created a feminist icon without understanding the nationalist role that she played in Mexico, and within the revolutionary movement.

bell: Each of our journeys have paralleled her journey. She was radicalized by an activism that is about decolonization, her questioning of imperialism, and her engagement in various political movements for social justice. And her politicization began around the question of class, not around the question of gender; she was most concerned about who gets to learn and who does not, of who gets to eat and who does not. So I think that it's ironic that she has been "chosen" by unenlightened white feminists to occupy an exalted space in their feminist pantheon, because these white feminists usually cannot deal with class issues. I mean, you take a woman of color artist whose political being is founded in Marxist and Socialist thinking, who is in correspondence with Emma Goldman and other radicals throughout her life, and then you turn her into someone who is all about stylistic rebellion! You level her curiosities and intellect into sexual scandals about whether she is or is not a lesbian, and how and why she and her partner fought.

The last photo taken of Frida shows her in her wheelchair, protesting at a demonstration against the US intervention in Guatemala in 1954. She has one leg amputated, she is in a wheelchair, she is pale and drawn, and this is the last thing she wants to be able to do. So there was always in her a struggle between her own, I think, desires for love and continuity and home, and her immense need to paint a reality that some call magical. I remember there's a quote from Breton or one of the surrealists describing her paintings as bombs wrapped in tissue, and tied with a ribbon. They told her that her works were surrealist and magical. And she would say "No, they are the reality of Mexico." In life, Frida Kahlo grappled with how she would define herself in the midst of imposed definitions, and this continues after her death.

And the cultural encounters which shaped her perceptions and art were encounters with indigenous people—peasants, farm-workerw—and her upper-class sensibility. Kahlo rejected preoc-cupations with manners and ladylike behavior—her identification with working people nurtured her defiance—but she had been steeped in this sensibility as a young person.

When she met Diego Rivera, this cultural encounter sur-faced again. And they had political differences, not simply romantic differences. Their tensions and conflicts were fueled by questions about where each will stand politically; who will each stand with; and, like all of us, what mistakes they've made. Most importantly, they had to try to correct these mistakes while remaining con-nected as partners and artists.

Amalia: And remember, he was significantly older than she was. This was his third marriage and he'd travelled extensively, so he wanted different things from the relationship than she did. But for me, Frida also embodied a bridge between the Chicano movement, which I participated in during the 1960s and 1970s, and the Mexicanidad movement of the 1930s. These two periods emerged out of great civil strife, and they were also moments of political and cultural transformation. During Mexicanidad, which came after the Mexican revolution, people like José Vasconcellos, the Minister of Culture, and others were conceptualizing *la raza cósmica*, or the cosmic race, by the 1930s. They were engaging in very broad and philosophic notions of identity as a nation and as individuals who were artists. So in some fundamental ways, there are parallels between these two movements.

bell: Well, let's start at the beginning. How do you find out about Frida Kahlo? Where does it begin for you? How old were you?

Amalia: So it's 1975, so I must be 32. By that time, Rupert Garcia and Renee Xanez were also working with her images. I went to Mexico City, where exhibits in honor of the International Year of the Woman were showing. For the first time they had an exhibit of Mexican women painters, and there was work by Remedios Barros, Maria Izquierda—all of these women I'd never known existed—and there was Frida. Then I went to her blue house at Coyoacán, and I remember having to leave the house to go out into the garden because I was so overcome, and I didn't want people to see me crying.

Each time we would go into another room, I would leave and sit on the little patio where Rivera had constructed this mini-Aztec temple. I sat near it, and had this enormous realization that she had this life with this man, and that her house had all her artifacts. For example, her original diaries were there then, you could see them. There was her jewelry, her bed, her body cast. And there was something so revolutionary about being in the presence of this woman who'd overcome obstacles related to physical deformity and disability, and who'd survived the sexual crises of unrequited love. Each time, she would rise above it.

That was the beginning of my connection with her. I did a little altar for her in honor of her birthday in 1975 in the window of the Galería de la Raza in San Francisco. In 1976, I did my first large scale altar, and she was one of the figures in it. In 1977, I created an altar for her and Diego at the Fifth Sun Exhibit at the University Museum in Berkeley, California. In 1978, we were collectively working with Frida Kahlo through the Galería. Carmen Lomas Garza, Maria Pinedo and I interviewed many women about their relationships with Frida, and we started to work on a book, but we were never able to finish it. Yet this opened another door—we decided that we needed to educate our own young people about her legacy.

We began to go to places like Stanford, San Jose State, UC Berkeley. We went wherever anyone would invite us, and we'd share what we knew about her. This project eventually resulted in a Day of the Dead exhibition dedicated to Frida. And this was the first time, in 1978, that a group of Chicano artists created works of art around Frida Kahlo, and her life. And the night of the opening Hayden Herrera came. She knew the work that we were doing, or she had heard about it. Ironically Hayden Herrera, who is not a Latina, attended this show. Her husband ran a notable New York magazine at the time, and they had tremendous access to Mexico. In her biography on Frida, which became the basis of the film with Salma Hayek, Herrera relied heavily on the work of Raquel Tibol. But Raquel Tibol interviewed Frida Kahlo in the last two years of her life, when she was completely sedated and in enormous pain; some have said she was delusional. So I have always believed that many of stories that have circulated about Frida are other people's fantasies, variations of the exotic savage narrative. This isn't the whole picture.

bell: I actually came to Frida Kahlo's work through my fascination with Diego Rivera's art. From my childhood, I have wanted to know more about the lives of farmworkers and share-croppers, because of my paternal grandfather's experiences as a sharecropper. So when I came to Diego Rivera's art, in my late teens, I was moved. Here was someone who felt that laborers and other invisible people were worthy of representation; and for me, his representations seemed to deify and bring out the sacredness of their work. In this way, Rivera reminds me of Sam Doyle, an artist who works in the folk tradition of the Georgia Sea Islands, and who paints portraits of everyday people. He created a public gallery in his yard, and his work is about transfiguration, the idea that you paint someone to illuminate their divine qualities. Rather than seeing portraiture as representation, the portrait was perceived to be a representation of the divine self.

I learned about Diego Rivera's life, then I learned about Frida Kahlo. For her, the portrait represents a complete journey into the self, into the Jungian concept of the collective uncon-scious that requires a recognition of the shadow self. As therapists like James Hillman describe it, the darker spirit resides within all of us. And Frida Kahlo was engaged in a kind of archaeology of the spirit; that is what we see when we look at her work. Were we able to put all of her work in one place and walk through it, we would see soul work taking place, through her self-reflection and her self-invention.

Amalia: Yes, because when you look at the paintings and arrange them chronologically, you have a parallel chronology of the events in her life. You see that there are moments when she relied on the paintings to take her beyond the limits of her own experiences, and they are transfigurations. And there are times in he life when she shows you the signs of her own suffering; her hair is wrapped around her neck, and the ribbons are tightened. Then there are times where she has surrounded herself with familiar figures of love, home, and intimacy—her little dog, the monkey. These are paintings where she is situated, she has all of her belongings with her, and she is home.

bell: There are critics who try to place Kahlo solely within the realm of magical realism. This does an injustice to the deeper, psychoanalytic dimensions of Kahlo's work, and it's an attempt to reinvent her, an attempt—through a kind of Western cultural imperialism—to situate her in yet another construction of the "primitive," rather than honor the incredible, intellectual, and politicized consciousness that was at play in her work, as well as her psyche.

Amalia: Like the painting based on Sigmund Freud's book *Moses and Monotheism*, which was called *Birth of Moses*. But it's a tiny, tiny painting, and she has arranged it so that it looks like ovaries, fallopian tubes, and the uterus, but it's really all of the iconography of sort of mythic and historical figures layered through all of it. If you don't know *Moses and Monotheism*, you would not know what she was pursuing. And I think it was more than an intellectual preoccupation. She is was one of the first and most powerful artists to interrogate the body as a site of turmoil and transformation; she constantly questioned that space between the living and the dead. There are elements in her paintings that literally no one else has ever captured. She represents her own birth, and even the iconography of the pre-Columbian era, as layered by a biological gaze, almost as if she were viewing it through a doctor's eyes, as if she were looking through a microscope. I think this comes from working with her father, who was a photographer, for years.

bell: She is an artist who has not been given her fair due. She's been reduced to a surface, to the surface image, which one can look at and say, "Oh, magical realism" or, "Oh, Mexican primitive." Very few people have seen her as a woman who received an education in critical consciousness that was not only along the lines of the most sophisticated political theory going, but who also was familiar with psychoanalytic theory. She was completely ahead of her time! Many women of color who are artists, writers and other cultural workers are only now discovering how valuable psychoanalytic tools are, because those tools have been withheld from us, and marked off-limits.

So it's important to talk about the erasures that occur based how we are framed and seen in the dominant culture. We're back to the question of representation because Frida Kahlo's image has become "domesticated," across lines of class, race, and sexual preference. People buy Frida Kahlo postcards, Frida Kahlo buttons...

Amalia: Earrings, T-shirts, everything.

bell: On one hand, she is probably the most widely recognized woman of color artist in the United States, but the way she is represented undermines the artistic scope of her work.

Amalia: We can go right back to cultural strip-mining. Her image has been commodified, marketed, and appropriated. But the irony of all ironies is that some Mexican intellectuals have charged us—Chicanas and Chicana artists—with trivializing Frida, and have called us opportunists for using her in our work. We've had to stand up and say, "Do you really believe, in this United States of America, that a handful of Chicanas could market an icon in this way? Have we published the books? Have we produced the posters? Are we selling the card sets at the Museum of Modern Art?" No. That's being done by wealthy and connected white women and men who have used her image for profit.

Raquel Tibol, who wrote one of the most pivotal books on Frida, actually challenged Chicanas in a public setting with profiting from Frida. This showed me how large the gap is between some Mexican intellectuals and some Chicana intellectuals. And many of these women are of European descent, even though they are Mexican by nationality. I think it must have seemed easy to challenge us, and never question white feminists about their relationship to Frida.

This seems connected to your observations about how Angela Davis has been marginalized, and how Winnie Mandela has been turned into a murderer. It has been relatively easy for people to make Frida so ubiquitous that she's almost invisible. What's happened to her image shows us how we need to be vigilant about our own self-representations because she's been robbed of her complexity.

bell: What do we do, though, with that trivialization? How do we disrupt it? For example, Malcolm X is a comparable icon. At one point, he was the leader that everybody identified with in popular culture—the cool leader, the hip leader. But just as very few people seem to know a great deal about Frida Kahlo as an artist, very few folks understand what Malcolm X was doing politically, especially at the end of his life. Just as Frida Kahlo is frozen in the moment of her relationship to Diego Rivera, Malcolm X gets frozen within the Nation of Islam, and what's not seen is his global consciousness—his radical leftist political consciousness—that develops and blossoms deeply and fully.

I don't know how you felt, but initially I was not excited when everybody was getting on the Frida Kahlo bandwagon. I felt that my private mentor figure, who'd inspired me tremendously, was now "open to the public." And I'd "earned" my relationship to Frida Kahlo; I had studied her life and work. But I encounter many dewy-eyed, young, white feminists who worship her but don't have any interest in that kind of work; they're not interested in paying homage to her, because they don't understand her value.

For example, I remember my first women's studies class at Stanford, when there was a conflict when one of the white woman students was talking about the Black maid at her home, and how much they loved her. And I raised the question, "But does she love you? What do you really know of what she says about you when she is home? What have you done to earn the right to talk about her?" Of course, I remembered that when my mother came home, the critique that she brought to bear on the white people that she worked for was *fierce*. They would not have been able to imagine it. She would come home and do a gendered critique, or do a critique of the idea of female freedom, of the white female leisure-class model in a way that the white people she worked for did not see because of their racism and classism.

Within cultural imperialism, unaware white folks learn that they don't have to study Frida Kahlo to "claim" her. Through the trope of cultural imperialism, they can impose intimacy. But it is the familiarity of the oppressor, the familiarity of the colonizer, where you push yourself close through violation. It's an aggressive desire, rooted in envy.

Amalia: I embraced Frida at a time when I was figuring out how to sustain my own individuality with my married partner, who was another creative person who needed his own space and individuality. I also went through that whole realization that I would be unable to have children. And I remember the sense of this closeness with Frida, because I had interviewed many of the people who knew her and they would sing the songs for me that she had taught them. They were old, and they knew her as friends, and so the stories they told me were nothing like the stories in Hayden Herrera's or Raquel Tibol's books. They were about her at her home, about how she arranged flowers, her way of cooking for people, her ribald sense of humor, and the vulgar songs she'd loved to sing to them. This was the Frida that I carried around with me.

Right around the time I had my hysterectomy, I visited the San Francisco Art Institute because Rivera had painted there, and she had been with him when he was there painting. She was breaking with him then, and had her show at the Julian Levy Gallery in New York. I found an old copy of the *New Yorker* with an image she had painted. I couldn't control myself, I took the picture home with me and put it in a frame. I put the picture on the night stand next to me at the hospital, and when I came out of the anesthesia I was very uncomfortable. I remember one of the Filipino nurses came in and she asked me what Santa this was, which Mexican saint, and I told her, "Oh yes, this is Santa Frida." And she was very impressed, and told me she thought she was very beautiful. And so from that point on, this "deification" became a secret and funny touchpoint for me.

One of the things I learned in all the years of working on Frida is she had layers of history with people. This community of women—María Felíx, Dolores del Río, Josephine Baker, Rosa Covarrubias—knew her and cared for her. I don't think they all had relationships with her, but each of them loved her in some form or another. You know, she was a woman's woman, a woman you'd want to be with because she could take care of things. There's a famous story about her. She was in New York, and Noguchi had an apartment in Brooklyn, and they were all there one night, a whole group of them, and they were making like a little home movie. And there was a rose—a play on the rose of Brooklyn, similar to the tree in Brooklyn. So they had the rose on the table, and everybody had to do something with it, so everyone concocted, you know, smelling the rose, and such. But Frida asked for a little piece of paper and a string, and she got a pencil and made a little card that has the letters "F.W." She punched two holes in the card, tied the string around her hips so that the "F.W." was on her rear end, and she danced with her butt wiggling around the rose. So everyone said "Well, what does that mean?" And she just looked at them and she said, "I'm a fucking wonder." She was an inventive and challenging person but, at a moment's notice if you were sick or if something as wrong, she would be the first person to come and bring you soup. So she has all these elements, I think, that have not made it into the movies or the books.

bell: In my book on art, *Art on My Mind: Visual Politics*, I examine the need for resisting representations. Another figure, a literary figure whose fate is similar to Frida Kahlo is Zora Neale

Hurston. Many people are laying claim to these women of color, who occupy complex positionalities, and simplifying them. They are claiming them in ways which deny their complexity. It's the white explorer who goes native to find their primitivism in the dark other—Gauguin goes to people of color to paint—but then who minimalizes their culture, reducing it. Margaret Mead goes to other countries, represents herself as a friend to colored people. Yet she calls the people monkeys in her journal. Even as white folks attempt to appropriate, utilize, and celebrate the art of the dark other, as subjects, they often maintain the hierarchy of the white cultural imperialist. Both Hurston and Kahlo have fallen into that gap, where their complexity can be lost in the reifications of their images.

Amalia: The white world engages in an embrace, but it's like the "embrace of death." A loving-to-death of the thing they want.

bell: To me this is a constant issue. How can we refuse this embrace and recover this lost value? As a woman of color, I needed to discover the relationship between Diego Rivera and Frida Kahlo, see her power within that bond, and observe the way they constructed the home, allowing for their autonomy and individuality. As a young woman writing feminist books, these artists of color were powerful icons. Diego Rivera taught me to see and embrace the beauty in working-class culture. Frida Kahlo showed me that a woman could be disciplined and passionate about her work.

And it is so compelling that she found a way to create art, even in the midst of great physical suffering. We're still living in a culture where women of color, much more than white women, still bear an enormous sense of guilt and selfishness when we put work—our individual work—first. This is especially true if it's art or intellectual labor. If we put jobs that earn us money first, people may understand that. But if you're putting something intangible first, it's hard for people to understand.

This may have something to do with why so few people of color write about art. For me, this writing has generated the least reward, financially and critically. In the past, you and I have talked about Lucy Lippard, someone whose work we appreciate. At the same time, we recognize that she automatically is more visible than people of color writing about art.

Amalia: It's as though when we write about our own experiences, or about one another, that we're participating in something that is self-serving and provincial. But when a white writer like Lucy Lippard does this, she is applauded for stepping outside her own experiences. If individual people of color are experts around their own histories and experiences, it means nothing. "Oh, of course, what's the big deal." This is so uneven.

bell: When we come back to Frida Kahlo, this even more true. If we could collect all the critical and personal writing about Frida Kahlo, most of it would be authored by white reformist feminists. This is one reason its great to have a dialogue about Frida Kahlo with you; this cross-cultural dialogue rarely happens. No one else is interested to know what Frida Kahlo to women of color, who she speaks to on that intimate experiential level—not as a symbol.

During my childhood I suffered a lot with asthma, and since then I have faced other health dilemmas. So I resonate with Frida Kahlo being in pain, and working through pain. For instance, my menstrual cycles were terribly painful. I had crippling periods from twelve-years-old on; I was really brought under by them. From fundamentalist Christianity, I had also inherited the sense that the female body is tainted, soiled, and sinful. Then, my female body suffered. I always felt that my body was letting me down.

In the wonderful film that Sofia Coppola directed called *The Virgin Suicides*, one of the sisters tries to kill herself. She's thirteen, she ends up in the hospital, and the doctor says, "You know, you're too full of life to be here. You shouldn't be here." And she says, "You have no idea how painful it is to be a girl."

Many girls have experienced that transition from girlhood into menstrual adolescence as traumatic in ways we haven't really been able to name. For many of us, it was a transition from freedom in our bodies to a sense of being enslaved to the body. Also in terms then, of the body becoming this "thing" that adult men prey upon. Early on, female bodies are in pain, and it is a big issue that's not often talked about. If we look, for example, at the way in which people have written about Van Gogh, and his own capacity to continue to work in the midst of psychological suffering that was often compounded by physical suffering through self-mutilation, we see a sophisticated analysis. We know Van Gogh now would be described as a cutter, a self-mutilator. We understand cutting now, but rarely in relation to the production of art. For him, there was a merging of a religion, guilt, and purging in the act.

We see this idealization of pain and suppression in Frida Kahlo as well. We have also come to see that women of color suffer disproportionately from many illnesses—such as lupus and various forms of cancer—but no one is invested in our physical well-being. And when women of color physically suffer, most of us have to go to work anyway; we're talking about farmworkers, factory workers, domestics, and women in other service industries. When I think of being in such severe pain that you just want to die, as Frida Kahlo was, we know the power of her imagination is what allowed her to go forward, and this must be true for many women. The fact that she could lie in bed and have these terrorizing dreams—the dreams that come when your body is seeking psychic release—and then utilize them as sources for her art, we know there was an awesome creativity there. There's no way to understand this through the colonized mind, which does not allow for subtleties, contradictions, and complexities.

Amalia: Yes, yes, yes, yes, you're right.

bell: And of course, fundamentally, what is needed is a de-colonized imagination that is not racist, that does not have a kind of reformist, boring feminist perspective. We need see her complexity of Frida Kahlo in the field of desire, in the world of art making.

Amalia: You've addressed this in your love trilogy, and I think another way to make that choice is to witness Frida and Diego's community, and witness whether they respected each other. Often people talk about the power issues in their relationship instead.

bell: And that is really sad, because we always struggle around power, even when we're deeply, passionately, truly in love. I've written a great deal about violence and antiviolence, but in the past, I have also been enraged at a lover and have responded violently. Somebody looking at that from the outside could just say, "Well, bell hooks is a hypocrite. She doesn't live out the truth of her words," instead of acknowledging that all of us live within contradiction. I'm not always controlled; I'm not always correct; I'm not always kind; however I can name and take responsibility for transgressions. I can change, I can make amends, and I can repair. These things that happen in relationship, and people looking at it from the outside in cannot chart the course of reparations, of reconciliations, because we usually can't see those things.

Amalia: Yes, that's not given as public view. I've never been candid about the private reasons that I was drawn to Kahlo. At that stage in my life, I was married and struggling to decide whether or not to have children. Then I discovered that I couldn't. And I found some resonances in Frida's relationship to Diego and my relationship to Richard. It was reassuring to see how two strong people with artistic temperaments who love each other will also have ambitions and dispositions and struggles that inevitably will invite conflict.

I like your word "reparation," because it's often obscured in Frida's and Diego's relationship. What I know from my own life with Richard is that people who love each other passionately can hurt each other. This can be resolved by believing and understanding that something larger than personal habits and emotions is often at work in relationship. For us, it was our shared love of beauty, of the making of culture; this held us together even as we sometimes failed each other personally and privately.

When Diego was with her in the Mexicanidad Movement, he was creating his pre-Colombian collection at the Museo de Anhuacelli, she was retrieving the exvoto or retablo (paintings on tin) and they were supporting and liberating artists who made the Judas figures, the papier mâché figures that the Linares family made. At the same time, they were brutally battling each other and Diego betrays her with her sister and belittles her over her other relationships, they are building this intellectual and cultural material that transforms Mexican society. There is something else that pulls them to rise above their pettiness, that allows them to repair and resurrect their love.

RESISTANCE PEDAGOGIES

bell: Many university scholars and tenured faculty act as if nothing connects them to public schools, where you spent twenty years teaching. This experience seems to have played a significant role in your self-development, self-actualization, and self-empowerment as an artist and activist. I chose to do work in the public schools because I recognized that all of the critical thinking we do in the university has little meaning for many people of color if it does not begin in the earlier stages of our educational development.

Amalia: The fact that my own education in many respects failed to capture my imagination, failed to recognize me in all of my capacities, and was unreceptive to me as a learner, was a reason that I was drawn to public education. As I grew older, I struggled for years and years to make up for those lost years.

bell: You've talked about what you thought being a student entailed—it felt as if you had to be assimilated into the dominant white paradigm. In a sense you awakened your consciousness later, during graduate school. You reeducated yourself, pursued your activism, and entered the public school system in San Francisco, determined to be an advocate for people of color.

Amalia: During the late 1960s, I was working with artists and thinkers whose primary goals were to serve the community. We looked around to see what was needed. First, I thought about working in a community school, and then I realized that most people of color were not in private schools or community schools—they were in working-class families, so revolutionary education had to happen in the public schools. I went through Teacher Corps, a program that prepared teachers to work in city schools. I began working in the Mission District then, and I spent twenty years in the public school system in San Francisco.

One of the most important teaching experiences for me was working in an open classroom. It was exhilarating to watch children learn without borders and boundaries, learn out of their imaginations, and provide them with information and lessons relevant to their life experiences. The open classroom had portable greenhouses, portable kitchens, and libraries. Students could learn science, math, and literature in a hands-on way, integrating learning at their own pace through their own experiences.

One of the concepts we used to develop literacy was "$E + T = M$, *Experience plus Text equals Meaning*." "Experience" was the life of the students, what they brought in the door. Now we call it "funds of knowledge" or "assets-based learning." It was based on the understanding that no learner comes to you empty. They come filled with their own experiences, the knowledge their families have shared with them, and the aptitudes they have gained in their own communities. The "text" is the teacher—whatever she uses, whether a book, a film, or a field trip—the teacher is the text. The goal is to apply knowledge to develop meaning—relevant and useful education that engages the learner.

For example, I spent many years teaching in San Francisco while a court-ordered desegregation plan was enforced. I was the first teacher to develop a professional development program for educators in schools that were being integrated. This meant that we had to confront recalcitrant teachers, people who did not intend or ever want to teach "those children." So to teach these teachers, I had to reeducate myself. I found that there was an enormous amount of critical pedagogy—such as cooperative learning, cultural learning styles, conflict resolution—that I had to acquire in order to prepare others. Our cultural differences made the experience more textured and richer, and we could base our response to diversity on the assets students brought.

It became apparent to me how much our educational system prizes individualistic, competitive, and isolated learning, and teachers had been trained to see that as a successful model. Interactive, hands-on, and collaborative learning had little value. So when a Black student engaged the material in his own style of communication and learning, if he called out to others in the room and they would respond to him, "yes, um hmm, that's okay, yeah, you go on," the white teacher would perceive that as acting out, get afraid in the classroom, and try to control it. And inevitably, ironically, the student who was most engaged with the material, would be the student who was the most punished.

bell: This clash was at the core of the "Ebonics" controversy in the 1990s. Young people were allowed to be engaged with pedagogy on their own terms and allowed to use what I would call the language of their intimacy, which can be simultaneously empowering and comforting. Let's face it—coming into the classroom initially is a threatening experience. And if you're not white and you've never had a friendly interaction with a white person, to come into the classroom and face a white teacher can be disabling or shattering. Having the freedom, the basic right, to speak in the language of one's intimacy allows new students to feel that they can belong, that they do not have to be alienated.

As a rural kid who had to travel miles to school, I initially expressed tremendous grief. It was frightening to me to go so far away from the private space, the only learning place I had known, into the public school system. I can't imagine what it would have been like to make that journey to people who would then treat you as though you were "other." I went to country schools where Black teachers welcomed my presence and spoke to me in my familiar language. It is so important for people to understand that the desire to be able to begin teaching in the vernacular was not an attack on our need to know standard English. It was in fact like a preparation of the soil.

Some of the most positive interventions that the Black Panther Party made in Oakland and the Bay Area were in primary school education—first, acknowledging that children first needed to have breakfast before school because they could not learn if they were hungry, and second, that literacy was crucial for their development. The Black Panther Party used Paolo Freire's approaches from *Pedagogy of the Oppressed* to educate young Black people, by recognizing that everything begins with literacy. Yet since that time, no social justice movement in the US has prioritized literacy. This is in spite of the fact that 1 in 7 Americans are functionally illiterate, and the number is growing.

Amalia: And Black and Latino students are still coming into unreceptive classrooms.

bell: In fact, this situation has worsened because of the governmental assault on public education. In the last fifteen years, through defunding, voucher programs, and the promotion of religious schools, our government has begun the privatization of the public school system. Education is perceived increasingly as something that should take place in the private school, in church, and in the governed school. The public school is becoming a holding camp, a kind of symbolic concentration camp before prison, and many of us see a return of racial apartheid with regards to public education. For example, the elementary school I attended didn't have a library or many other resources that were "givens" at privileged white schools, and this kind of inequity is on the rise today. Jonathan Kozol powerfully documents this trend in his new book, *The Shame of the Nation: The Restoration of Apartheid Schooling in America.*

Amalia: And special education has a special relationship to prison. Many black boys in public schools are tracked from kindergarten straight on through middle school in special education classes. They don't exit until they hit adolescence, and then many of them make their way into the courts and prisons.

But with a more critical pedagogy and strong bilingual programs, we could respond to these challenges. There are opportunities to transform these young people into the teachers who might reenter the public schools and transform them. In fact, the absence of white students actually makes it easier for us to construct pedagogies that are more relevant to our youth. One of the things that happens to many Latino students who have come here from Mexico and Central America, is that they must confront this *rechazo*, or in Spanish, a rejection. In their own country, they've become used to teachers who greet them each morning with a kiss on the cheek or a hug. They're used to having personal relationships to the authority figures in their school, but here teachers beyond the third grade are not allowed to demonstrate affection or intimacy towards their students. These students come into classrooms where teachers don't even remember their names, where the classes are so overcrowded that they haven't even got sufficient resources.

Yet this juncture, where we are in the process of educating first-generation students in settings where all of the students are young people of color, gives us spaces to transform pedagogy.

bell: You're describing a potential field of resistance, but we also have to talk about school systems like the one in Flint, Michigan, where my sister Gwenda teaches and where I occasionally work. The teachers and students are overwhelmingly Black, still the overcrowding is so bad that the effective pedagogy you are talking about could not be fully implemented because there are just too many people. And throughout my years as a teacher, I have found that if you have one determined troublemaker, whether it is in the third-grade classroom or the graduate seminar, it can ruin a class. And if you have larger numbers it becomes harder to control. How do we deal with that effectively?

Amalia: I guess this approach and this desire comes from my public school experiences, which I have brought into higher education. Before I came to California State University at Monterey Bay, I had never taught in university. I had been a visiting scholar, a regents professor, an artist-in-residence, but I learned to teach in actual public school classrooms, and I actually find that the same things work here.

For example we are currently dealing with the need to scale up and teach larger classes. In order to teach a class of fifty-five students, I have to build classes within a class; or, collaborative and cooperative models based on the concept of a team. The entire class is divided into teams of eight to ten students, and each assumes a role working on research, presentation, or visual materials—everyone has an opportunity to contribute.

Each team presents to their peers and the instructor, and this is what brings the course content to life and gives each student a chance to apply and master the material.

bell: You have described a model of engaged pedagogy that works and encourages critical thinking. But what fascinates me is that teachers are not prepared on the primary, secondary, or college level to teach in the diverse classroom. They are, for the most part, not trained to be critical thinkers. Much of the failure in the university nonbias curricula was due to the fact that teachers were not trained to teach in the diverse classroom. First, they had to unlearn all the things that they had learned for ten to twenty years. Let's just deal with the basics in grade school: Columbus discovered America. Most teachers have been saying that for twenty-five years. How do you get them to change their thinking and honor the presence of indigenous people here before Columbus, and just as importantly, tell the truth about Columbus's conquest and colonization.

Amalia: You have to foster scholarship. In one of my graduate courses, we give students two chapters from a book called *Thrown Among Strangers: The Making of Mexican Culture in Frontier California* by Douglas Monroy. They finish reading that, and excerpts from something called *Red Eyes*, which examines curriculum to look at the positioning of American Indians, and every single one of these liberal arts students who are preparing to become teachers write tearful essays about how they feel cheated, and how they are in a rage against their teachers. How could they have reached college and discovered realities no one ever told them about? They feel betrayed by the educational system, but I believe that reason the grade school teachers didn't assign *Thrown Among Strangers* is that they've never read it. If we were to cut teachers some time loose to develop reading circles so they could develop their own scholarship, I think some of them would transform their curricula immediately.

When I was running staff development in San Francisco, there was a moment where ethnic literature was being introduced in the tenth grade for the first time. We got very angry letters from people saying, "I have always taught Shakespeare and I don't see why I have to teach this." So we set up a reading circle for every single high school, and we provided the books for free. We brought in authors like Amy Tan, Gary Soto, and others to meet teachers and to discuss the stories with them. And they went away completely transformed. They simply never even knew where these books were. They never had the time to go get the books, never had the time to read them, and had no one to talk with about them. Once they had read and enjoyed the books, they were inspired and confident enough to teach the literature.

bell: But look in states like Nebraska, Oklahoma, and Texas—big states that have major control over the content of textbooks. In primary and secondary schools, we're seeing increasing levels of censorship. There is a growing resistance to the idea of teaching writers who bring in different perspectives. This censorship is quite widespread, but it does not always enter the mainstream media, so people do not know that there are libraries in Wyoming, Montana, Nebraska, Oklahoma, Texas, where people are taking books by people of color out of the library and reinstating a biased perspective.

Even as a student at an all-Black school prior to integration, if I wanted to read Black writers, I would have to go to the library and hunt those Black books down on my own. Once we integrated schools, so many of my white teachers were telling me that Black people didn't write, I stole a book called *American Negro*

Poetry from the library. I wanted proof that there were Black people who wrote, so I could show those white teachers who said, "There are no Black writers." And you know there are university and college campuses today where white professors continue saying we read no Black writers, we read no Latino writers, because they haven't written anything of quality or depth.

Of course the greatest interventions have been made on the college and university level, and I want to speak about this for a minute. We have different pedagogies for those who are perceived to be in line to become members of the future ruling classes. Among the white folk and small numbers of people of color who are being educated at the so-called Ivy League schools, or top-notch schools, it is recognized that if they are working with China, Japan, Thailand, all the different cities and nations of Africa, they must understand diversity. They must learn something about the mores of other groups of people, so for these few, diverse education has become a commodity deemed essential to business as usual. Yet this appreciation of the need to learn about other cultures is often not seen as vital at the community college or public university.

On the other hand, if we go into community colleges, we find hostility to bilingual education. We don't have teachers telling Black children, "If you really want to have a work future in America, learning Spanish is essential." We don't find Latino students earning extra credit because they enter college knowing two languages. Yet there are many, many places in our nation where speaking Spanish determines whether you get a job or not. And many of these jobs will be taken by those privileged white kids who were encouraged to learn Spanish.

Amalia: And Latino kids are being forced to forget Spanish and learn English, so that they will have fewer options. There has been tremendous hostility to bilingual education in California, Massachusetts, and throughout the Midwest. Some of that is about the education industry.

As you mentioned, there are states where textbook adoption is big business, with state guidelines for every discipline or subject area. There is the textbook industry, in regular touch with local school boards. State textbooks are like what Hallmark would be to poetry. They are deluded and reduced reality, and we give them to young people and wonder why they don't learn to read! And for the last twenty to twenty-five years, conservatives have positioned themselves to take over school boards and assume authority over curricula, removing books and teachers. Finally, there is the unwavering emphasis on testing, with George Bush and his "No Child Left Behind" cronies at the top. People are teaching toward the test because the test is the dominant measure and scores supposedly show whether or not they're being successful. So this quantifying of education robs us of the quality of the experience of learning. This approach has been devastating to the arts since they are not testable disciplines—music and visual art have nearly dropped off the radar, and are virtually nonexistent in the high school curriculum.

For example, phonics is a huge industry. Now instead of talking about compelling and motivating literature itself, and emphasizing sight reading, contextually, and beautiful excellent illustrations, many kids are spelling words out, and that's it. I'm not opposed to phonics, but there is an industry now around a certain type of literacy and a certain type of reading, and all of the new moves that Bush is making in education, that is "vocational." We've gone through a period in California under Wilson, Deukmajian, and now Schwarzenegger where the revisions to state guidelines on teaching history were really an inch short of racist. We had to battle, and are still battling, to get the state guidelines in the arts to sustain arts education. After Proposition 13, it disappeared from public schools in California. The change in the funding base has destabilized arts teaching in California's public schools, as there are no art teachers in the primary grades and limited arts education in high schools.

bell: We've both talked about how the art classes we were able to take as public school students were a major part of allowing us to enter that space, particularly as kids from working-class homes. My theory is that people in power don't want art to be an ac-

cessible resource in the schools because of the consequences of art
making in the last age of multiculturalism. The work of Basquiat,
Carrie Mae Weems, and Lyle Ashton Harris are fine examples of
this, of the way art became a vehicle to narrate struggles and demands for marginalized people. Art-making provides a process
for us to explore our life experiences—including the experiences
of prejudice, racism, and homophobia—and make them public.
It follows that art is now perceived differently than before—it is
seen as a vehicle for change, as a force that can break down the
boundaries and expose inequalities. So, people of color and the
poor are denied access to art for fear that if they get their hands
on it, they'll write their own stories and understand the value of
their lives. Let's expand that, not just to art, but to education as a
whole.

Amalia: This is true. And when I reflect on my develop-
ment as an artist and intellectual, it's clear to me that Affirmative
Action played a huge role. Without it, I would never have gone to
Stanford. I would have had to attend college closer to home, where
I might never have been recognized as a thinker by my teachers.
Affirmative Action came under assault because it has been a suc-
cess, not because it's been a failure.

It's important to remember that much of the change that
occurred on US campuses in the 1960s occurred because Black
people were insisting on access to education with such an intensity
that many of us came to awareness. My own political awakening
happened in my first year of college when I read *The Autobiography of
Malcolm X* for my Black studies class. Look at Angela Davis, Alice
Walker, and Toni Cade Bambara—so many people from working-class backgrounds were able to develop critical consciousness
in conservative institutions. Despite many obstacles, Affirmative
Action created an educated class of nonwhite people. So, it's no
accident that we have a backlash. And today, there's not only an
assault on Affirmative Action but on Women's studies, Black studies, Chicana studies, and so forth.

bell: I agree. The discourses on democracy, diversity, and civil rights in this country have often taken place on a philosophical level, but the moment they're engaged in forcing change, and in forcing power to change hands and generating agency for nonwhites, people stop and say, "Well, we really don't need to do that because we have already accomplished that." In other words, we've already talked about it—we don't need to do it. As you've said, Affirmative Action was about doing it. It was about making choices about resources. Yet, many young people of color believed they didn't need Affirmative Action until it was actually taken away. Now you see students really insisting that these programs be preserved. There have been protests and other campaigns foregrounding student demands that the university find ways to provide support for students of color *and* working-class students.

Amalia: I there has been a huge mystification around Affirmative Action. For instance, the programs in elementary schools that identified young women and people of color who might be interested in science careers weren't always paying their way into Yale or Stanford. These programs were baby steps.

On a related note, I'd like to return to language. People like Shelby Steele and Richard Rodriguez are people of color brought into certain discourses as regulators. They've fulfilled their duties, so we don't hear from those individuals today.

One of the first places where Richard Rodriguez's book, *Hunger of Memory*, was distributed was in the educational journal of the teachers' union. Some of the chapters were included in a series of teachers' union publications at the same time that bilingual education was being challenged. The whole of the teachers' union had turned their back on bilingual education, largely because it privileged the experience and the expertise of teachers of color who were not the primary constituency of the union leadership.

So this writer allowed his work to be used to dismantle bilingual education, and to put up an obstacle against Affirmative Action. Richard Rodriguez *knew* he never would have been in the places he had been in if not for Affirmative Action, and that he had practiced his own Affirmative Action. And he disguised his struggles as a gay man of color within other contexts. For instance, when he talks about his disenfranchisement, his discomfort with his family, it wasn't only because he was a dark-skinned Mexican. That was certainly part of it. But what he was really talking about was the rupture, crisis, and alienation of his own interior and secret life, and how that had never been understood. So he mixed the two experiences of being gay and being a man of color but called it culture, or "ethnicity."

bell: But he made that choice for a reason, which is related to how celebrity, fame, and reward are constructed. I've been told by people that if I would take a conservative position—like come out against welfare or Affirmative Action—then I would have certain kinds of approval from the dominant culture. As people of color, we know the greater the degree of your assimilation, the greater your reward. We are all vulnerable to that seduction, and people like Shelby Steele, Richard Rodriguez, Dinesh D'Souza, and Ward Connerly have been acting it out.

Here are people who are clever thinkers, but nothing special. They haven't produced bodies of work that required people to take note of them, so it was the only way they could jump the organic hierarchy. And once they did their jobs and became the people of color who came out against Affirmative Action, they could be dismissed. Now we don't need a Shelby Steele, because the white male voices are well in place and they could say things without being seen as racist because they can refer to the work of Richard Rodriguez, Shelby Steele, and James McWhorter. This also made it hard for people of color to respond, because so many of us feel we must be careful when we critique another person of color.

Amalia: In the 1990s, Connerly was the major figure in the anti-Affirmative Action campaign within the University of California system. As a Black man who had earned his points with all the conservatives, he led the charge. And who could question a Black man saying that Affirmative Action crippled Black people? Eventually, even his own family made remarks about him fleeing from his Blackness, and that made no difference. He was able to carry out his crusade against Affirmative Action and have it dismantled in California. Then he took it to other states! Only a Black man could have done that...

bell: Even more exciting for the state of California if a Chicano man had done it...

Amalia: And look at Linda Chavez, who was Bush's first choice for Secretary of Labor in his first administration. If she hadn't been harboring undocumented immigrants in near-slave conditions, she probably would have been appointed. As these people continue to emerge as powerful political forces, the question will be whether or not we have counterleadership. That's one of the dilemmas right now—where is the leadership in education? Where is the leadership in terms of cultural resources? Where is the leadership in our communities? In the current Bush administration, archconservatives like Alberto Gonzales—who supports legal torture for detainees and wiretapping of Americans—are out in front. Since César Chávez, no public figure has galvanized the emotional and political commitments of large numbers of Chicanos. For Chicanos in particular, these are very important questions.

bell: Part of that crisis enrages me, Amalia, because it seems to be a crisis of gender. For example, you are charismatic, you are brilliant, you are courageous, and you love justice. There's no reason you shouldn't be one of the leaders you're talking about, but what we find imprinted again and again on the consciousness of Black and Latino people is that we must have male leaders. We can be sitting in the midst of powerful visionaries, still people will not follow them.

I often think about Angela Davis. She may not have wanted to lead masses of people during her lifetime, but if George Jackson had survived, it's hard to believe that he would not have been handed a mandate to lead. The people never really handed Angela Davis a mandate, because the dominant discourse privileges the endangered masculinity of men of color. Increasingly, that discourse devalues the wisdom, intellect, and leadership of women of color. People will act as though "Well, it's fine that we have all these good and powerful women, but we need real leaders…"

Amalia: When saving our men, who are endangered and at risk, comes at the expense of extinguishing women's opportunities, we continue to endanger our communities.

bell: One of the issues that I've worked with in the public school system and in university classes is preparing Black men to receive knowledge—knowledge that will enhance their ability to fully and deeply live—from women. And to get there, we have to work through so much sexist conditioning. They've been encouraged to negate the resources women are willing to share with them, so they have to undergo a feminist conversion to appreciate and utilize the wisdom that women teachers, family members, and coworkers offer them. And it's amazing to me that more and more Black men I know of are doing this. Enlightened Black men all over the nation are saying to me, "Why should I continually mourn the loss of Malcolm X and stay stuck when thinking women are capable of leading me in the direction of freedom?" And I think that's the kind of revolution we need. In the other direction, there's this ongoing conservative emphasis on special schools for Black boys.

Amalia: Military schools.

bell: Yes. Education for Black boys is infused with imperialism. The message is Black boys must learn discipline and punishment from grade school so they will be prepared to be disciplined killers for the nation—not gangsters out in the street, but to be the soldiers that Bush can send to Iraq or Iran. I think this is true for Latino men too. Whenever we talk about pedagogy and kids of color, we have to talk about liberatory education. We have to talk about the fact that while many Black children need discipline, they can learn discipline in Montessori schools, they can learn discipline in open classrooms like the ones you ran in San Francisco. They can learn discipline in all kinds of ways. Militarism is not the only way to learn discipline. Punishment is not the only way to learn discipline.

Many men who have had a military or militaristic education conduct themselves with great dignity and honor in public space, and then go home and abuse and emotionally shame their families. For them, there is no connection between their capacity to conduct themselves ethically and honorably outside the home and their violent and abusive behavior in intimate relationships. This seems important to say because so many Black folk are seduced by the boot-camp education, military-base education propaganda for young Black men. The thinking is that this education will prepare them to be responsible patriarchs. If we don't call this into question and interrogate it, one day we may see state-funded boot-camp schools for Black boys, in place of public schools, that will be mandatory. Essentially they'll be reform schools, but they won't be called that. In fact they will be legislated as an alternative to prison. So we'd better wake up and return to the public school as the site of revolution, return to what the Panthers knew with great wisdom: we must be educated for critical consciousness on the primary school level. Not when one is twenty, not when one is eighteen, but when one is learning how to read and write.

Amalia: These schools are an extension of our own internalized racisms. We have learned to believe that we produce young men who are violent, impulsive, and out of control from the outset, and the only way to educate them is to externally control and punish them. But if we know anything about human development, we know that discipline is supported by our ability to make our own choices, and by our understanding of the relationship between cause and effect. A person doesn't learn to be disciplined through punishment and manipulation and fear. Unless we create a pedagogy that offers young people in their homes and in their schools opportunities to make decisions and respects their judgment, they won't be able to do it.

When I started the regeneration project at Galería de la Raza, it was our first attempt to develop new Chicana leadership in the service of our communities. We recruited young Latino artists, eighteen to thirty-six years old, and invited them to work-shops and gatherings in San Francisco many years ago. We went in thinking it was an intergenerational project, including artists like Judy Baca, Carmen Lomas Garza, Ester Hernández and oth-ers, thinking that we had something that we could give them. It was true they wanted our stories, but more than anything they wanted our watchful presence as elders. Once we were there, they would have the courage then to take the project and turn it into something that they wanted. They created their own exhibitions, they created their own salons, they created their own online zines, they created their own afterschool programs, they created their own arts education curriculum. They only needed our respect and our invitation and our watchful presence, and once that was given, they could move forward.

What I saw in this new generation was mixed-race Chicanas, gays and lesbians, middle-class Chicanas and Chicanos who didn't look the way we did, but who still wanted so much to be a part of that process. And all we had to do was simply be pres-ent for them and they'd have the courage to do the next step. But if we don't have that belief in them, and that respect for them, they won't be able to do it. Not only will they have to resist the larger white society, they will have to resist us because we've refused to see what is possible in them, and they will have to teach us at a great cost.

bell: Or they will continue to feel that they have to erase and dominate us in the name of colonized white supremacist thinking. Essentially, we are talking about the difference between a pedagogy of the oppressed, and the continued pedagogy of genocide.

PUBLIC CULTURE

Amalia: People have always asked me, "Why do you call it visual and public art, why don't you just call it visual art, or why don't you call it public art, why do you say both?" And if we simply say "visual art," people might think that we mean the individual production of objects of beauty. If we say "public art," they might think that we mean only those things that were large, big, and outsize. In order for us to develop a language about artists working in public settings, we must start to talk about making public culture.

We've talked about public culture, and it overlaps somewhat with popular culture. We could be talking about film, landscapes, murals, or about collective endeavors and celebrations like "Day of the Dead." We could be talking about museums that receive public funds, but we usually perceive them as privatized entities. So if we can talk about public culture, we're talking about what we mean by "culture." And we have been burdened for many years with a word that begins with a capital *C*, a well as a dominant master narrative that we usually have no place in. Instead, we have small cultures with little *c*'s—Chicano culture, Black culture.

bell: Where did you even begin to think about culture? As a southern Black girl in a working-class family, I don't think I ever really heard anyone talk about culture. Where did it enter your life?

Amalia: In my Mexican life, people would often say *nuestra cultura*, or our culture. They weren't talking about necessarily fine art work, but about how one behaves, one's worldviews, the importance of respectful relationships between people. For me, public culture has always had social dimensions.

bell: In my southern upbringing, the culture I learned about was "high," not "low" culture. I was taught that European culture—Western white classical music, the theater, opera, all of those things—were the things that educated people knew about.

Amalia: This was also a part of my experience. For example, when my mother went to clean at the house of well-to-do people who worked in the Navy at Moffett Field, in what is now Silicon Valley, they gave us their castoffs. Sometimes we'd get things like a slightly chipped but otherwise perfect perfume flask, and I would fill it with water so I could smell the perfume. I knew that there was another world that was "cultured," but I felt somewhat alienated from it, and didn't draw as from it.

bell: As a child, I my parents made sure I left the small town I was raised in to visit a museum, but when I came to Los Angeles for the first time in my twenties, I was shocked to meet many Black folks who had never visited a museum, even though they lived within walking distance of one.

Amalia: This is one of the questions we have been interrogating for a number of years—how do public institutions become privatized? Why are poor or working-class people uncomfortable going into museums? After all, all of us pay taxes to keep museums open. This was one of the big "multicultural" struggles—challenging the museum, a privatized site, to become more open and public.

And obviously, free or cheap media is an element of public culture. We've both discussed the profound manipulation of images of women of color—particularly in advertising and on television—and how distinctions between pornography and mainstream representations of women have been quite blurred.

bell: The engine behind it all is capitalism, which demands that everything be accessible and available to all consumers. For instance, I remember the first time I was wandering through an airport and I stumbled across a Victoria's Secret store, with all of the sexy and revealing underwear in the displays. And I'm wondering, who *needs* Victoria's Secret in the airport, you know? In the displays, the visual blurs the distinction between public and private. It subtly evokes the pornographic gaze, which is usually a private and secret pleasure. Now capitalism urges us all to cultivate a pornographic gaze—we're all invited to look. There is no longer a sense that only pornographers look at women, desire women, and long to violate and mutilate women. Some of us understand that we live in a rape culture where all of us are encouraged to be symbolic pornographers.

This is also what MTV is doing, and they have a long reach. And if you look at the trajectory of young, Black (or ethnically indeterminate—Black female bodies have practically disappeared from the screen) female bodies, the biracial body is idealized. The light-skinned colored woman with long straight hair is identified by patriarchal pornographers as the ideal sex object.

Asian women are also being objectified—just look at "crossover" films like *Memoirs of a Geisha, Charlie's Angels,* and *Crouching Tiger, Hidden Dragon.* Despite the useful and eye-opening discussions of racism and white imperialism, much of it provoked by Edward Said's *Orientalism* and other texts, people now talk openly about Asian women as being "in vogue," as though there has never been a critique of this racist and sexist objectification.

For example, several years ago Wesley Snipes was interviewed in *Ebony,* and he revealed that he prefers Asian women over Black women because, "they know how to serve." On top of trafficking in disgusting stereotypes, the moment he says this publicly he pits Asian women against Black women in an economy that is sexist, misogynist, and pornographic. And unenlightened women can think they should be fighting one another for the privilege of "serving" him. It's this kind of pornographic and racialized sexism that has become the norm.

We see this again in the movie *Sideways*, where Sandra Oh is portrayed as a drug-using, sexually promiscuous, single mother with a dark-skinned Black child.

Amalia: This takes me back to Jennifer Lopez. One of Jessica Alba's parents is Mexican, and she's being constructed in a similar way. They're both mixed-race Latinas, but they are usually marketed as white or white Latinas. However, they're not completely deracialized; they never *completely* "pass." People may not have not recognized Jennifer Lopez as an ethnically black Puerto Rican, but like other Black women, all this attention was paid to her ass. She was made into a contemporary Hottentot, and this happened because Black culture has been usurped. I know you've said the Black booty has become too familiar, too cliché. I'm not sure if the Black booty is "over," but this kind of objectification is multiplying and shifting.

bell: One of the messages is that colored women cannot enter public culture if we are not willing to sell or commodify our bodies, whether as sexual objects or as servants. Or both.

Amalia: The laboring body.

bell: Indeed. We can never *not* be represented as the laboring body. No matter what role we play, we must be workers. Even though people can say we have more Latinos on TV or in the movies, these images are constructed within racist, sexist iconography. There are rarely counterhegemonic characters or situations. I don't know how many people saw *The Mexican*—it came out a few years ago—but I thought it was very, very interesting. It had moments of radical intervention. Within the movie, there was a critique of white supremacist culture, of the racist and sexist ways that white Americans see the country, yet the trailers for the movie emphasized the notion of white supremacy in relationship to Mexico. Ironically, this movie actually challenges much of white cultural imperialism at the border, with incredible scenes. For example, there's a scene where all the different white men are talking about the car that they want as "authentically" Mexican, as the Mexican men are making fun of them in Spanish.

But the trailer told me to stay away—I felt that I didn't need to see yet another sort of racist representation of Mexicans. But then someone told me that I should see the movie. I wondered whether the producers of this film thought if they really showed people what the movie was about that they wouldn't go see it. In this case, racism was a marketing tool: they didn't want to tell us that the movie challenges racism. Instead, it seemed like it reproduced the same old racist stereotypes.

We have to constantly critique imperialist white supremacist patriarchal culture because it is so normalized by mass media and rendered unproblematic. The products of mass media offer the tools of the new pedagogy. Most of our mass culture comes to us in television and movies because increasingly people feel afraid to leave their homes and to go into unfamiliar neighborhoods or spaces, like museums. Also, people don't have disposable income for culture. They want to encounter the other in a space where they have control over the image. You can delight in the image of the bad gangsta Black man on your screen then express racialized fear when encountering real Black men in daily life.

Amalia: We might also talk about censorship as it relates to race and representation. For example, in the last fifteen years, the National Endowment of the Arts has nearly collapsed under the burden of censorship. And this "governmental" proclivity has touched and infected society at large. One of the things I've looked at is how public art is being blocked, and who decides what art goes into what community. We're talking about pre-censorship, with regards to public art.

bell: As you were talking about what art gets into which community, I was thinking that our communities and neighborhoods should have their own centers, with art galleries to celebrate the art history of the people who live there, as well as educate people from outside of those communities. This would be a way to make culture accessible.

Amalia: I used to believe that public art could be a source of transformative power to people interested in social change, that it would allow marginalized communities to document and record their stories. But over the last fifteen years or so, we've witnessed intense and strident battles about control and censorship in the public space.

A great example of this is the controversy that surrounded Noni Olabisi's "To Protect and Serve," a mural about the history of the Black Panther Party. At my university, in the class "Ways of Seeing," we teach the story around Olibisi's project. The mural was met with the most enormous resistance by LA council members, and they were able to constrain and control decision making, and prevent public funding of the art. Private funding finally had to be raised to complete and install the piece.

Obviously, there are other ways that artists are censored, and in some cases, we unknowingly participate in censorship. For example, an artist is commissioned to build a gate for a big city park, ostensibly to secure the entrance and exit. Actually, officials want to close off that space and prevent entry to homeless people and other "undesirables." For some city officials, "beautification" means eliminating all evidence of homelessness and poverty from public spaces—governments think that these are disfiguring elements in the visual landscape, and municipal and departments and art commissions are following in lockstep. So artists can inadvertently become involved in surveillance and social control.

Many years ago, I was invited to give a talk on public art to a conference in Los Angeles at the Biltmore Hotel. For those of you who don't know, the Biltmore faces a large open area called Pershing Square. Pershing was an Indian killer and a Mexican hater, besides being a general. The city contracted a well-known Mexican architect, Ricardo Legrorreta, to design a public piece for Pershing Square. They recruited a Mexican to build an homage to a Mexican hater, and it included a series of colored walls that allow the hotel and other corporate landowners near the square to close themselves off from Mexicans on the other side of the square. There are big questions about the economics and politics of public art, and whether or not it can serve the community, because artists are helping government and corporate entities control, rather than liberate, space.

bell: But artists aren't the only marginalized folks controlling real estate. Think about the colonizing role that wealthy white gay men have played in communities of color; they're often the first group to gentrify poor and working-class neighborhoods. Harlem is a good example. Gays have moved in and driven up rents, as have renegade young white students, who want to be cool and hip. This is colonization, postcolonial-style. After all, the people who are "sent back" to recover the territory are always those who don't mind associating with the colored people! And it's a double bind, because some of these people could be allies. Some gay white men are proactive about racism, even while being entrepreneurial. But in the end, they take the spaces, redo them, sell them for a certain amount of money, while the people who have been there are displaced.

And in some cases, the people of color who are there are perceived as enemies by white newcomers. When I was at a fancy restaurant in San Francisco, white people were saying to the owner of the restaurant, "We don't want to be waited on by somebody who has an accent." They had come to dine in the Mission, a neighborhood where people of color live, but they openly displayed their racism and white supremacy. Ironically, the white European owner had an accent, but it was acceptable.

We really see this watching what's going on in Harlem; we're watching the community as we know it disappear. One of the first acts in the white appropriation of Harlem was eliminating the African marketplace, a site of public culture. Street vendors didn't just bring their products, they brought homemade artistry, whether it was food, music, or crafts. So when the state eliminates street vendors, they take away public culture. They begin the process of colonizing that territory, making it not visibly Black.

One day, Harlem will not have much to do with real Black people—the representation of the community as a "Black mecca" will be used solely to sell products. In my neighborhood, the West Village, rich white heterosexual families are moving in and saying,

"This neighborhood is too gay, we don't want to see certain things on the street." And of course we're all thinking, why did you come here in the first place, if you don't want to see certain things on the street? But the point is, they have the money and the power within public culture. They have the police and the mayor behind them, so they can change the nature of this neighborhood.

Again, this raises the issue of who owns public culture, who is it for? Prior to Katrina, New Orleans had a huge black population, and a thriving black culture. That's gone. It's been destroyed, and racist white people are glad. They want just enough public blackness for tourists, and no more. The "new" rebuilt New Orleans will not be infused with the history and flavors of the Black diaspora, and it will not be a center of Black power.

Amalia: I think the big questions may be who owns public space, who shapes the space, and how is the public space defined? Sometimes I use Los Angeles as an example, because the city has a very important history for Mexicans in particular in respect to place making. In the late 1700s, the majority of the city founders of Los Angeles were actually either descendants of Africans, mixed-race people, or indigenous. Only a handful of Mexican people helped to found the city of Los Angeles. Yet "El Pueblo de Nuestra Señora la Reina de los Angeles del Río de Porciúncula" is the name that is given to this place.

Fastforward many years, to the twentieth century, and redevelopment is underway in LA. Sonoratown is bulldozed, and Chavez Ravine, a very historic barrio, is evacuated so Dodger Stadium can be built. After that, Bunker Hill, another Mexican neighborhood, is relocated for a music center to be built. As Los Angeles has been redeveloped, huge numbers of Mexicans have been relocated and displaced. But the past cannot be completely erased. Every place is haunted by those who lived there first.

I appreciate art theorists like Edward Soja and Henri LeFebre and others, because they explore how innocent landscapes really disguise relations of dominance and power, and once you look into the space, you can find who has lived there before. On the surface, there are all of these false histories and dichotomies in art, public culture, public space. As people of color, many of us know what real stories are, so we can usually see what's going on just below.

bell: Think about it—people of color—how many times do we enter a bank or a library, any place that has an image that assaults our being? It's probably not an "innocent landscape," but another image that is playing on our hypervisibility or on our invisibility within the dominant culture. How many times do we feel that we have the right to talk with the person who decided to place the image here? Usually, we feel that we are powerless in the face of the image. While our art and artists are censored, we don't feel that we have the right to question choices about what images are used in public spaces.

As we talk, I'm realizing how many censorship cases involving people of color have interfaced religion and sexuality. In our society, religion has been a force that domesticates and subordinates people of color, and this is increasingly true in the first part of the twentieth century. For example, racist patriarchal interpretations of Christianity are pervasive and influence the lives of people of color. Look at the traditional Black church, and the role it has played in conservatizing and colonizing Black people. All over the world fundamentalist Christianity is used to keep people of color subordinated. And as the Christian right's use of and presence in the media continues to climb, they're not having problems with diversity—Blacks and Latinos are joining with them, spewing hatred toward gays and lesbians and supporting the war and other forms of fascism and repression.

Yet it is an ironic moment, as far as representation, religion, and politics are concerned. In the US, there's a lot of talk about changing demographics and the growing Latino population. Bush has a few colored people in his cabinet. But most of these right-wingers, across class, support regressive and punitive immigration legislation, and oppose bilingual education. It's obvious that power dynamics are not fundamentally changing, in spite of the numerical shifts. As long as our nation refuses to support bilingual education, for instance, we're in fact supporting the status quo: the creation and maintenance of a servant class for white imperialist capitalist patriarchies. That's all it will mean, unless we begin to have some fierce revolution around literacy.

In fact, we must acknowledge that if we don't have a mass effort toward literacy, all we are doing is reproducing a transgressive yet elite body of individually privileged Black, Latino, Asian and Native American thinkers, artists, and writers who are set apart from the communities they come from. That's what we have to be constantly working against.

Amalia: Many of my friends and I chose to teach at my university because it was the first institution that said, "Diversity is central to our mission." California State at Monterey Bay is committed to serving under-represented students, the working poor, and first-generation college students, and they are thrown into company with students from other backgrounds, so driving down Blanca Road—the "white road" between the campus and Salinas—we have some awareness that new opportunities have been opened up here for the servant class you were talking about earlier.

But wisdom about resistance, resiliency, and compassion doesn't always come from books. These are things that many working-class and poor people know about, intimately. In Spanish, when someone doesn't behave, we'll say *es mal educado*. It doesn't mean they don't have enough degrees or formal education, it means they don't know how to treat other people. They don't have "home training." Literacy is essential, but it's not the only thing that you need to see you through in life.

bell: It's not the only way of knowing. In my book on class, *Where We Stand: Class Matters*, I write about what a difference it would make if we were to see the poor as guides, as people we can learn from. For example, look at the "living simple" and "living with less" trends in the mainstream. The people in our nation who are *forced* to live daily with less are the poor, yet we disparage them instead of holding them in high esteem for their resourcefulness.

The prevailing image of the poor in mass media is still of a criminal class, certainly not a teaching class.

In that sense, mainstream culture tells us daily that the poor have nothing to offer. And it just reminds me again of a world in which the slaves are creating the wealth and yet we're being told that Black people are lazy.

Amalia: There's also the image of the sleeping Mexican.

bell: Indeed. In the dominant, capitalist culture, the people who are laboring the most also must endure representations of them as unworthy, lazy, and poor by choice.

Amalia: Mexicans are the human food chain. We plant it, we grow it, we harvest it, we truck it, we prepare it, we cook it, we serve it, and we clean it up after. Despite the absolute necessity of our work, we're still seen as thieves, as criminals. And many of us are completely vulnerable, because we don't have the same citizenship rights. Working in Monterey Bay, I routinely drive down the white road, and every time I look out my car window, I see migrant workers in the fields. And it brings up feelings of guilt, anger, relief, and respect, all at the same time, because they are doing something my parents did, but that I don't have to do. They work under unforgivable conditions to feed us, but they cannot get fair housing.

When I was young, my parents and I would take rides to a nearby beach. Now my parents live with me, and I take them for the same ride. We have to pay to enter the same place where we once freely drove, the 17 Mile Drive in Pebble Beach, as it's now a private beach for the wealthy. But all I have to do is drive down the white road to see another group of people who lack the resources for adequate housing and recreation.

bell: They cannot have private lives, because as workers, as the new slaves, their lives are not their own.

Amalia: Exactly. And they live their private lives in public.

bell: When you think about slavery—Black folks could not use the bathroom, choose their clothing or where they lived—it becomes very clear that there's a kind of slavery taking place today. It was named by some of the demonstrators against the racist and punitive immigration laws that are being pushed by conservatives. We're living in a plantation economy and within a plantation culture, and that makes me reflect more on the nature of displacement and homelessness.

For example, I believe African Americans were the first "homeless" people in this nation. I should clarify: indigenous people will always *know* this land is theirs, and that it belongs to them, despite the fact that it was forcibly taken from them. But after slavery was abolished, millions of displaced African-descended people had no homes to return to. Lately, I've been writing about the circularity of that homelessness, and how this displacement is happening again. All over the nation, the state is closing housing projects and more and more Black people are being put out. And no one asks, "Where do the people go?"

When Cabrini-Green, an enormous project in Chicago, was closed, newspaper and magazine articles featured people reflecting on how terrible the conditions were, and what a positive thing it was that the homes would be destroyed. Not one article called attention to the fact that people received relocation notices that they had to act on within a week—they had to get out, and they were not always assigned new housing somewhere. If your family missed the notice and did not relocate, you were just without a home. Now, in the aftermath of Hurricane Katrina, we are witnessing the wholesale creation of homelessness, largely Black homelessness, by the state. And who is calling attention to the racialized, gendered nature of this homelessness? Certainly not white male leaders.

Everywhere I go, people talk about the dearth of leadership. They ask, "We're in crisis, where are our leaders?" And I say all the time, "There are plenty of leaders in our community. They are women." And until we are able to end the sexism of Black and Latino men, we will not benefit from that leadership. Many people, male and female, are not willing to follow a woman leader.

As a positive celebration and a challenge, we need to highlight the reality that female leadership is the future. We are the possibilities of a new world, a humane world, a just world. And in our physical embodiment we, I think, offer the promise of renewal, of a world where women like us can come to power. While we can realistically face the limitations imposed by sexism and racism, we can also celebrate the struggles and victories that have brought us here. You and I are part of the joy there is in antiracist struggle, the joy of moving past the misogyny in our individual lives so we can flourish as women artists.

And that takes us back to the issue of class and privilege. Privilege is not in and of itself bad; what matters is what we do with privilege. I want to live in a world where all women have access to education, and all women can earn PhD's, if they so desire. Privilege does not have to be negative, but we have to share our resources and take direction about how to use our privilege in ways that empower those who lack it. Let's talk about reciprocal education, not just reciprocal art. Let's talk about sharing conversation as a radical act.

MULTICULTURALISM

bell: As we've discussed, multiculturalism was first introduced into the business world in the US, long before a progressive discourse about diversity had began in colleges, universities, and other institutions. Businesses started diversity workshops because the US was losing business in Japan and other places. Unlike the Europeans, white Americans did not know the proper rituals and codes, and they hadn't bothered to really learn them.

The business world, the capitalist world, was the first major force in this country to recognize the importance of learning about "different cultures." They said, "If we know the cultural codes we can then exploit them for profit. We can have ads that show dark people with blond people. We can use this whole diversity thing to our advantage." Yet when multiculturalism arrived in the academy, white people were much more hostile to it—particularly unenlightened white people who didn't see any advantage to having a multicultural perspective.

Amalia: I experienced how this impulse shaped public education as the 1960s were coming to an end. Various multicultural curricula were being advanced, but they were still really very superficial celebrations. We used to say if we keep this up we're going to have a lot of fat and happy children who can dance.

bell: Because they've eaten the foods from all the different countries of the world!

Amalia: Right. This superficial multiculturalism was aided and abetted by shallow multicultural education in the public schools. This is separate from the advances made by the university scholars who confronted the unenlightened white folks—the teacher-activists who were behind the development of programs in African-American studies; Latino studies; Asian American studies; Native American studies; gay and lesbian studies; and women's studies have made profound and lasting contributions.

But what is not clear to me, even though I was a participant and a witness to it, is how multiculturalism has shaped the mainstream arts and entertainment worlds in the last twenty years. Do you think these changes are connected to the business enterprises of diversity training?

bell: Absolutely. Remember, we are now dealing a class of white elites who were radicalized by, or at least exposed to, the movements of the 1960s and 1970s. They're not like the capitalists before them. Many have become fiscal conservatives, but many remain social liberals. Instead of being afraid of the ghetto, some of these folks were the white folks who wanted to go live in the ghetto! Some of them took on the trappings of being Black, or of being another kind of "other," so as businesspeople they're not afraid of the "other." Instead, for them, black and brown peoples represent a gold mine. This was a big shift in white supremacist entrepreneurial capitalist mentality. As the children and young adults of the 1960s occupy the seats of power, return to white supremacist capitalist patriarchy, and become the CEOs, they're not as afraid of Blackness. They are simply more prepared to exploit and market it.

It's not surprising that young white males—most between thirty and forty—play major roles in the production of hip-hop. It's easy to forget this because when most people critique rap and hip-hop harshly, they assume that young black men are the sole creators and producers of misogynist rap. In fact, nothing is unilaterally produced anymore. As we've discussed, once you have a corporate takeover of the street culture, it is no longer the property of the young, Black and Latino men and women who have created it. It is reinvented with the mass consumer audience in mind. The hard-core misogyny and the hard-core sexism isn't a translation from street to big-time studio, it is a *product* of the big-time studio.

Amalia: Our vantage points are really different on the evolution of multiculturalism. I was an activist within the Chicano movement in the late 1960s and 1970s, then I worked in community-based institutions and entered Teacher Corps, a somewhat refined outreach program. I decided to teach for many years in the public schools, and I was a member of the first generation to bring a more radical brand of multiculturalism into the public schools in the 1970s and 1980s. This is the arc I reflect on.

bell: But we are talking about parallel occurrences. One does not negate the other. For instance, I could argue that the feminist movement alone didn't really propel women into the workforce; the state of the economy in the 1960s necessitated it. Pushing white women into the job market helped to maintain the lifestyle of the white middle class. But that does not diminish that the feminist movement provided the ideology that supported the women who chose to work outside of the home.

Amalia: Yes, because as you describe this multicultural trajectory, it ends with the mainstream media, an industry that is incredibly destructive to our communities. People are building community-based institutions, determining at one point that they're anti-elite but eventually coming to a conclusion that they also need to demand responsiveness from larger institutions. So I always think of what Amiri Baraka said: we must have self-determination, which is the building of our own institutions and the rights that exist within, *and* we must have democracy, which is our belief that our rights should be evidenced in the larger system.

We build community institutions, we create the art, we build educational programs and structures that some would call multicultural, and we go to the doors of the museum and we bang on the doors and say, "You need to respond to us." And they begin by providing us access. They take one painting, and then they take one show, but they never deliver the interpretive lens to us. It's similar to how you've described the corporate mentality. It finds radical material and co-opts it.

bell: It translates it into a consumer-based, not a politically based, multiculturalism. In the wake of the Black Power Movement, in the wake of Chicano and Chicana resistance, you get the backlash—let's get rid of Chicano studies, let's get rid of Black studies, but let's keep the consumerism. Let's all come to the table with our separate foods and tasting, as long as the white man or woman is still at the head of the table.

Amalia: I think one of the models for destructive advertising was set by the old, original Taco Bell "Run for the Border" campaign. In the 1990s, before NAFTA, Taco Bell started a marketing campaign with the slogan "Run for the Border." The first commercial was set in a fraternity house, with young men standing in the windows shouting, "Tacos! Tacos!" And then they ran, jumped in a convertible, and made a run for the "border." In the American imagination, the border is a place of transgression, prostitution, drugs, alcohol, and pleasure, now including junk food. After NAFTA passed, and relations with Mexico became more economically valuable, and the campaign was changed. It was called "Across the Border," because Mexico was seen as a legitimate neighbor, a partner in commerce.

Later, drawing on stereotypes like Frito the Bandito and the fiery, sexualized savage, they introduced Dinky, the Chihuahua. In one of the early commercials, Dinky sees another little dog—a dog in heat—in a flower shop window. He runs past her, and stops at the foot of a quasi-Latino man who looks down at him. And in the biggest Mexican voice you've ever heard, that little Chihuahua looks up and says, "Yo quiero tacos." Here we are animals, we are embodied in animal food, and we are consumed.

Over time, this campaign incorporated every negative stereotype of Latinos imaginable. And the scariest part is that we are now among Taco Bell's target audience. Latinos are now urged to consume a facsimile, a simulacrum of their own food, and eat their own destruction. They have forgotten their grandmother's recipes, taken in these smarmy advertisements that denigrate them, and consume the food as they consume the image. Their own culture is represented as disposable, as fast food…

bell: As worthless.

Amalia: Yes. The Taco Bell campaign has given way to more subtly insidious images as Latinos have become the largest ethnic group. But liquor ads still feature sexualized and racialized images of Latinas, selling tequila and everything else.

bell: The participation of Black cultural producers—many of them sexist, misogynist men in the entertainment industry—has given license to the ongoing production of racist and sexist iconography and racist and sexist images. In one of his older videos, Snoop Dogg turns everyone into a dog. Think about it—there was a cultural moment when African Americans would have been up in arms at the representation of Black maleness as bestial. This video said you're nothing, you're a dog, you're beneath my contempt. Yet because Snoop Doggy Dogg is acting in it, people can have the misguided belief that these images are coming from "the people."

More recently we have the Queen Latifah movies, the Nelly video where he runs a credit card down a woman's ass, anything with the Wayans brothers in it, and movies with Black men—like Tyler Perry, Martin Lawrence, Eddie Murphy—dressing in drag as Black women. These are all constructions drawing on and reinforcing stereotypes, and because of Black participation in generating these images, it's harder for people to figure out how to respond. If white males overtly were putting forward images of Black males as animals, or of Black men dressed up as mean Black women, it would be seen as so obviously racist, and Black people would get together and protect themselves against them. But when all manner of stereotyping and degrading images are created by Black producers, consumers often lack the awareness and the appropriate language to protest.

When I critique colonizing images of Black folks created by Black folk, people argue with me all the time, and tell me how Black people are "being paid." We're seeing more Black people in Hollywood than ever before. True. But what's amazing is the representations of Blackness are not evolving. They're no different than years ago, and in some cases they're worse. Now we're in a world where Black people say, yeah, it was really denigrating, but look how much money they got paid.

Then there are the movies and television shows with Black men impersonating Black women. These representations tap into a racist, sexist iconography that's existed from slavery on into the present day! That's why Sojourner Truth had to expose her breasts in the first place, to prove that she was a woman. This construction of Black femininity has been reinforced by propaganda like the Moynihan report in the 1960s, and mainstream patriarchal criticism of writers like Alice Walker, Michelle Wallace, and Ntozake Shange in the 1970s and 1980s.

Think about the wild popularity of Scheherazade Ali's book about Black women written for Black men, *The Black Man's Guide to the Black Woman*. Thankfully, the book is now out of print, but she argued that Black women needed to be put in their place by "their men," that we needed to be disciplined and punished, that sometimes we need to be hit. All that time, Ali was on the national television shows and interviewed everywhere. I watched conservative Black people and folks with plain common sense buy into the racist, sexist iconography that we used to oppose. Now we have popular television evangelists like T. D. Jakes imposing sexist puritanical notions of "right womanhood" on Black women, who eagerly consume these images.

The 1960s was the historical moment in Black life in the United States where there was a collective critique of stereotypical representations of Blackness. Then there was a slight improvement in representation in the 1970s. Yet today, many produced images harken back to the earliest racist and sexist images. Contrast the harmonious relationship between husband and wife on *The Cosby Show* to the images of Black husband and wife in the Academy Award–winning film *Crash*. In *Crash*, they verbally abuse one another showing hatred and contempt. And once again the Black "single mother" is assaulted and treated with contempt: she's a drug addict.

Traffic, another film celebrated by some people of color, draws on the same old images of Black men first presented by *Birth of a Nation*. The images of Black people and Mexicans—all are negative. Ironically, the white male pedophile is shown in a more positive light, a more positive representation than the Black male. On one hand, we have seen this hateful, unloving white family. We've seen the white boy who degrades this white girl by getting her addicted to drugs. However, the image of evil is the dark-skinned, naked Black man who goes to the door with a gun, whose erect dick and erect gun threaten—he is fearless. And this film portrays him as powerful, as the man in charge. This patriarchal, pornographic fantasy of race comes from the white male's imagination, because there is no such Black man. The cinema feeds the fantasy that Black men may have no money, they may be homeless, but they somehow have this power to control whiteness.

This is how white supremacy continues. It seduces everyone by producing false images. And yet these images have power. They help produce a culture where Black males are feared and hated. For example, many Black people in the age of multiculturalism support the death penalty. The fact that Black men are far more likely than any other group of people to be put to death doesn't sway Black people who are conservative. Like their recent counterparts, they believe Black men do not deserve to live. In the sixties, during militant protest, diversity and multiculturalism were radical terms.

Multiculturalism, as we define it today, came in response to movements for self-determination. Those movements were subverted and co-opted by the conservative state. Before Martin Luther King and Malcolm X were assassinated, they were talking about global imperialism, global technologies, and other hierarchies of power. They were critiquing imperialism and militarism. They were not limiting their critique to domestic racism. Late in his life, King spoke passionately about the need for Black people to oppose militarism, imperialism, consumerism. Had Malcolm lived, Farrakhan could not have come to power. Farrakhan is the embodiment of the militarist, misogynist, and capitalist ideology. Malcolm left the Nation of Islam to repudiate those things. But much of this has been forgotten. In the age of multiculturalism—not the age of self-determination—Farrakhan can be on the cover of *Newsweek* or *Time* and be presented as a "Black leader." Many Americans did not even know who he was until the mainstream (white) media gave him the backing, the representation that he needed to draw a wider audience. And together, they become the gatekeepers of the same old patriarchy.

We've seen that people of color who come to power within existing structures are usually not concerned with self-determination. Multiculturalism, much more than self-determination, invites liberal individualism. Conservative leaders like Colin Powell and Condoleezza Rice push the message of assimilation. And the liberal white world is just as quick as the conservative white world to tell us there is no racism. In his new book *Covering: The Hidden Assault on Our Civil Rights*, Kenji Yoshino, a gay Asian-American law professor, explores the push to assimilate. No one wants to talk about the way white supremacy is maintained by the state, by public policy. Multiculturalism says let's all have our own little cultures and fight for visibility.

Amalia: Before children are able to interact with each other, they engage in something called "parallel play." If you look at them in the sandbox, they appear to be playing with each other. But when you get up close, each child is in their own imaginary world, playing side by side. And that's what the conservative vision of multiculturalism is—parallel play.

This plays out in the art world in a myriad of ways. For example, often curators select pieces by people of color that will confront, scandalize and generally offend the majority of white viewers; this ensures that the work would not be seen again. And I don't think they did it for that purpose. I think that what happened, once again, is that whites could only understand our experiences in relationship to our perception of them. So that they picked work that they thought was about our understanding of whiteness. Once again, they were the primary subject—even in our own work.

bell: That is why we have to make distinctions between self-determination and increased representation. In the late 1990s, Clinton was willing to provide a national platform to talk about how racism doesn't serve the "common good," but there were no corresponding concrete efforts to challenge white supremacist thinking and behavior. Furthermore, Clinton's support of racist policies undermined his antiracist rhetoric. The Bush administration has been clearly reinscribed white supremacy, starting with the refusal to count Black votes in Florida in 2000.

Amalia: I agree. A different example of this dichotomy, with regards to government policy, dates back to the NEA censorship battles of the 1990s. When the dust settled and the agency had been downsized and defunded, the category for expansion arts—the source for smaller and more diverse art organizations—had been eliminated. These grants had supported community-based organizations, and organizations run by people of color. When this category was eliminated, small institutions like the Galería de la Raza in San Francisco ended up competing against the Museum of Modern Art for grant support. Many Latino organizations lost most of their financial support.

bell: Ironically, racial integration opened the gates for liberal multiculturalism, as well the kinds of government support you're talking about for people of color organizations and institutions. But when we talk about liberal multiculturalism, the people who move and shift are people of color, while whiteness stays in place, at the center. A radical multiculturalism demands that all parties shift their positions. So if we were practicing it in the primary education, the public schools would have to shift.

For example, it's been documented that white teachers show greater kindness to kids who they think are beautiful, and that those kids tend to be white and fair and straight-haired. We know that Black and Latino people suffer from internalized racism. So to teach toward a radical multiculturalism, white teachers would have to unlearn this racism and engage and nurture all the kids in their classroom. Along with the white teachers, we'd certainly have to work with the conservative people of color who are invested in the status quo. All of these practices are documented by Jonathan Kozol in his recent book, *The Shame of the Nation: The Restoration of Apartheid Schooling in America.*

Amalia: I think another way we move towards a radical multiculturalism is through engagement and dialogue. Most young people learn about cultural difference in the public schools as they are growing up. But we are still struggling to build educational enterprises where interethnic intimacy can grow, where we can choose to exchange our histories, our similarities, and our differences without it passing through the purifying, manipulating, and dominating centrality of whiteness. We are struggling with that now, as it's becoming more and more clear that our ability to build alliances is essential to our survival as people of color.

bell: And we've entered an especially dangerous political age where billions are spent on war, budgets for social programs are gutted, and where we are pitted against one another for limited resources. We need a place of cultural exchange where we can stand in solidarity and learn from each other.

Amalia: Given the divide-and-conquer narrative, it would be easy to think that as Latinos increase in numbers, Blacks will lose the role of the traditional minority in the US, white people are going to talk about Latino issues, and Latinos are going to have some greater number therefore some greater participation in institutions of power. This is a total myth. Ultimately, our numbers have little to do with the relations of power, but we're certainly being pitted against each other.

bell: Absolutely, and the sad thing is that many Black people are falling for it, forgetting that this notion of being a "favored minority" is itself a construction within white supremacy.

But most Black people know that while race is often talked about in black-and-white terms in America, that there has been no

sustained and sincere effort to change the position of Black people
in this country. If we were "favored," Black people would not be
getting poorer and poorer and poorer every year! Yet because the
racial rhetoric in this country has always operated on a black-white
binary, it's easy for nonblacks to see us as "favorites." I've heard
this from Latinos and Asians.

Amalia: For some people outside the black-white binary, it's
almost as though there have been two people in a room wrestling
with each other, fighting with each other for years on end, never
knowing there were other people in the room that were also being
beaten or being hurt. The language that we used about race and
racism has focused on black-white struggle, so there is a common
perception that the word "race" is a code for "Black." And that
"racism" is something that happens between Blacks and whites.

Latinos have always had a vexed relationship to this rhetoric. For example, the census has not assigned Latinos a separate
racial category. We are referred to as "Hispanics and other whites,"
so we fall into strange categories that are either "sort of ethnic"
or "sort of white," and we play out that game. There are many
Latinos who prefer to call themselves white. There are Chicanos
who prefer to call themselves Native. There are Latinos who call
themselves mixed-race. And now there is a small glimmering of
potential revolutionary change, with the increasing visibility of
Afro-Latino people, and the incorporation of Caribbean culture
into Latino studies.

When I try to imagine a hopeful philosophical place where
we could have the cultural exchange we've been talking about, it
would certainly involve taking on the mythology of race. And in
this moment of crisis, if we might find ways to excavate the histories and common struggles that Natives, Mexicans, and African-
descended people have had in the new world, then we might be
able to start this dialogue. We could stop seeing each other in
fictional categories that don't serve us.

bell: To have a progressive and radical multiculturalism,
there must be reeducation for critical consciousness. We have to

create a potential language that moves us beyond boundaries. The Black-skinned people who are Native Americans in this society certainly know that the dualistic categories "Black" and "white" don't work—so do many Black Puerto Ricans, Black Dominicans, and mixed-race people. With this intervention, these groups would be able to more freely articulate their lived reality with different politicized terminology.

It would be helpful if more radical folks would politicize and expand the category "Black," and use it as it's used in Britain. Sometimes when I've given a public talk, an Asian or a Latino person expresses concern about me using the categories "Black" and "white." And I ask them why don't they identify with the word "Black?" But I also understand that while they may feel that much of what I'm saying is true for them, they would like me to speak specifically to their experiences as Asians, Latinos, Native Americans, which is part of being politically accountable.

Within the economy of white supremacy, Black people have not been any more politically accountable than other groups. We haven't taken the time to learn about one another, or to examine our own. On a basic level, that means learning about one another cross-culturally. People of color become so focused on whiteness that we do not give each other respect and recognition.

You and I first met each other at "Show the Right Things," a university- and museum-based conference in New York City. That event was a positive example of institutionalized multiculturalism. Since then, I have not attended a conference that drew together so many people of color and white allies from various places in the world to talk. Today there are few forums that bring us together again, and ultimately when we really talk, when we really get the space, we have to be self-determining in creating it. We cannot rely on any existing mainstream institutions to bring us together.

Amalia: There are a few exceptions. From the late 1980s through the 1990s, Marta Moreno Vega from the Caribbean Cultural Center in New York City organized a series of gatherings called "Cultural Diversity through Cultural Grounding." They represented the major attempts to bring together people of color in a global construct; they were a powerful series of events where Native Americans, Asians, Latinos, South Asians, and African-descended people from all over the world all came together to network and learn from one another. And that's been the only enterprise I've been involved in that was nearly impossible to fund, and nearly impossible to organize.

I've worked other events involving museum approaches to diversity, and people threw money at us. We had no difficulty securing funding from foundations like Rockefeller or Ford, and Ivy League universities lined up with support as well. But when it came to creating a space where people of color could determine their own vocabularies and language of social change, few foundations were interested in giving us the money.

I've been thinking about the late John Ogbu, a sociologist who did pioneering work on what he called "voluntary" and "involuntary" minorities. Involuntary minorities are people who were either internally colonized, or brought here through slavery—Native Americans, indigenous groups that are mixed with the Spanish, Mexicans, African Americans, Chicanos, and Puerto Ricans are involuntary minorities. Voluntary minorities—Asian Americans, other Latin Americans who are not Chicanos—came under other circumstances, and for a purpose. And then he documents how a century or more later, involuntary minorities remain locked into the lower levels of the US economy, and how voluntary minorities, particularly Asian Americans and some groups of Latin Americans, have been more socioeconomically mobile. And as people come into this country and free themselves from indentured servitude or other forms of oppression, the temptation to identify with structures of power is too irresistible.

bell: They also create their own self-determining structures of power. There is an economy of Asian businesses in the United States that's unmatched by Chicano or Black wealth. Even though individual Black people are worthy members of the ruling class—Oprah Winfrey being the most obvious example—African Americans have little mass media we control. Under racial apartheid Black people had to build their own capitalist infrastructure, since whites wouldn't even sell to us. We had our own stores, our own doctors, dentists, and lawyers, our own schools, and our own entrepreneurs, like the businesspeople who went into hair-care products.

Today, we have a very sophisticated market-survey industry that tracks which products people of color buy, so the corporations can make money more efficiently. Now that mainstream publishers know we read, we can see the same thing happening with books for the "African-American market." But once again, the literature of Black self-determination is not what the white corporate publishing world decides to advance. Instead, it's trashy fiction that extols capitalism. Terry McMillan started the trend. Lynn Harris is a conservative Black gay man who writes novels about goods, cars, style, and the aesthetics of everyday life. His plots obsessively revolve around the houses his characters live in and the designer clothes they wear. A huge majority of his readers are straight Black women, even though these romances are about Black gay and bisexual men.

The common thread here is consumer capitalism. White CEOs and their minions can say we want to reach these markets. But let's not offer them messages to decolonize their minds; let's reach them by offering them the same old, same old, let's reinscribe the existing culture of imperialist white supremacist capitalism. The primary imports of the slave economy were salt, sugar, coffee, and tea—products that were all about addiction. The slave masters gave the global working-classes sugar so they could work them harder. To this day, more chocolate is eaten in Britain than anywhere else in the world! Let's give narcotics to the poor so they won't be able to have agency.

Amalia: Our communities tend to be very family-centered, as well as large and extended, but Latinos face the same encroachment into our lives by corporate America. For instance, the grocery industry in the Southwest knows more about Latinos than any research firm, educational institution, or mass media; they were the first to do serious consumer market analysis of Latinos in the US. They know what we consume and that we have product loyalty—if our mothers used Colgate, we will keep using it. They know that we consume more diapers than any other group. They know that we have the lowest median age in the country. As we have become a more visible group, wider consumer culture has begun to effectively market to us in Spanish-language media, as well as the English-speaking media.

And the term "Hispanic" has now become so pervasive that it is eliminating the heterogeneity of the larger Latino culture. One of the biggest behind-closed-door struggles happening in the Latino community has involved the prominence and power of the Cuban conservatives. They have played a huge role in funding conservative Republican candidates and have worked to maintain the Cuban embargo, while still having a more favored immigrant status than Mexicans.

So within the larger Latino population, there are enormous struggles over our identity, over relations of power and over the marketing of Latino identities. In some respects our conversations about multiculturalism are not about the museum exhibitions, or why Latinos are discovered every decade by yet another museum, or why we forget the power of artists like Matta Lam and their influence on people like Jackson Pollock and the modernists. We often end focusing on Latino celebrities, or popular culture, instead of literacy, representation, education, or economic enfranchisement.

bell: Sometimes, fear of being labeled "politically correct" leads people of color to refuse radical critiques of domination. Many people believe movements for self-determination in this country like Black Power or gay rights were about identity politics, when they were not. When we are committed to self-determination, we recognize that our lives are enhanced when we act in solidarity with other people of color and when we are able to recognize white people who are antiracist allies in struggle.

Most people in US society are confused about the meaning of self-determination. That's because identity-based politics does not demand radical political consciousness. For example, Afrocentrism is a conservative identity politics. It is rooted in fundamentalist religion—often Christianity or some form of fundamentalism like Afro-Caribbean Catholicism. This brand of identity politics is not progressive. And at the end of the day, we live in a society where white mainstream racist culture encourages our investments in these more conservative forms of identity politics. Once again, the example of Malcolm X is illustrative. He's assassinated at the moment when he is beginning to eschew identity politics and make connections between Black people in the United States, the Middle East, and Africa by Black folks who felt he should have had a more conservative focus. Farrakhan, who is a straight-up imperialist capitalist invested in a narrow and conservative notion of identity politics, does not need to be assassinated, as he can be manipulated by the imperialist white supremacist capitalist patriarchy.

Despite the hype, it's important to remind everyone that Black capitalism is not Black self-determination. Just as patriarchal white supremacist capitalism was willing to accept as many white women who wanted to climb on board, it is willing to accept as many Black males who are willing to climb on board. And while we don't have the local business infrastructures that Asian Americans have created, there is a visible class of wealthy Black elites, including Oprah Winfrey, Spike Lee, and Michael Jordan. And they are basically social liberals and fiscal conservatives. They are conservative in their politics. Despite the assaults of the Bush administration on all Blacks, poor, working, and middle-class—there is still a Black upper class, particularly in large cities like Charlotte, Atlanta, Chicago, Washington, D.C., Philadelphia, New York, and Los Angeles.

Facing the reality of class conflict among Black people reveals that our class interests are not always the same, and individual Black leaders find it more difficult to talk about self-determination. The class interests of poor Black people on welfare are much more linked to the class interests of Chicana and Chicano farmworkers than they are to the class interests of wealthy or middle-class Blacks. How do we then talk about Blackness? Ruling-class Black people often prefer an identity politics based on skin color, because this allows them to ignore their class privilege. As a result, rich conservative Black folks (celebrities and others) can feel comfortable trashing the Black poor—Bill Cosby is a prime example. He created his wealth by employing and appropriating elements of Black vernacular culture which he now talks about contemptuously.

In *Race Matters*, Cornel West opens his book with the story of how he can't get a taxi even though he's a Princeton professor. Of course, the lie of that is that those of us with money don't have to sweat it—we can call car services and limousines. But he still chooses to use that trope. Who is he using it for? He's not using it for the working-class Black readers, because they say, "Wait a minute, you can hire a car." But if you're speaking to white people, the image of the celebrated upper-class intellectual not being able to hail a cab can evoke sympathy.

Narrow identity politics remain the basis for political organizing because folks cannot handle the growing class divisions within our communities that are dividing us far more now than at any other time in American history. How do we talk about Black self-determination with ruling-class Black people? How do we talk about the sharing of resources?

Amalia: These issues around class differences are also something that Chicano elites—including movement leaders who survived the 1960s and 1970s—have trouble confronting. Some of this is about unresolved history, and guilt about the failures of the movement.

For example, in the 1960s and 1970s, many young Mexican activists were targeted by the state, and physically and psychologically devastated by state violence. Though it's not as well-known as Kent State shootings, the police violence following the National Chicano Moratorium March was a turning point. In August, 1970, more than 35,000 Latinos participated in a peaceful demonstration against the Vietnam War in Los Angeles. The police invaded the park, and beat and bludgeoned and killed people, including Ruben Salazar, the leading Chicano news reporter in the LA, and perhaps the country. Salazar was shot in the face—he was essentially assassinated—and a coroner's inquest ruled that the shooting had been a homicide, but the policeman involved was never prosecuted.

This was a moment of collective crisis, which the movement may still be recovering from, and then, the cultural wing took up the reins.

I saw myself as part of that wing. We attempted to realize our self-determination by founding our own institutions, such as the Galería de la Raza and the El Teatro Campesino, and have had our successes. But we did not anticipate the enormous influx of Mexicans who have come into the United States in the last thirty to thirty-five years. At this point, their needs are more similar to our parents than ours, in respect to labor conditions and housing. We didn't predict the changing power relations around the border. And we never imagined a NAFTA, which has allowed US companies to build factories and exploit workers in Mexico.

The Chicano community needs to determine how we can work with Latino leadership—mainly in labor unions—within the US, as well as with progressives in Mexico and Latin America. And we need to address the same kind of class divides you described in the Black community. We have begun to, and these dialogues have mostly been around immigration and labor, as the saving grace of Chicanos and Chicanas in the US is our history as labor activists. As a people, many of us are working-class, and we always fought for fair housing, fair working conditions, and fair pay. In some ways, this cuts through the mystifications and confusions around multiculturalism—working-class people certainly possess their own cultures and interests, but their first priority is to secure a living wage.

bell: This certainly contrasts with Black experience, where there has been a steady moving away from labor organizing as a source of political power and activism since the early 1960s. And we've also seen a complete devaluing of the politicized art created by working-class Black people, which was created by men and women from working-class backgrounds in the 1960s and 1970s. Young Black people don't know about this period or the work, because most of the art currently validated does not address the issue of class.

Even when contemporary gay Black male artists like Lyle Ashton Harris or Glenn Ligon make use of the Black male body, their work is seen by the mainstream art world as in the same tradition as Mapplethorpe. The Black male body is represented as isolated—and without community. It's an estranged body that stands alone.

Meanwhile, poor Black people are getting poorer every single day. And many Black people who have money are getting richer. Overall, the African American artist who makes it in the mainstream is increasingly seen as an individual with no connections to a larger community. Significantly, when individual Black artists and critics attempted to raise questions about Kara Walker's work, their voices were silenced. The hegemonic and racist white godfathers of the art world told her critics, "You have no right to raise these questions because we have selected this person. We feel that what she is doing is marvelous. How dare you raise critiques about it!" Walker, in her own right, deplores an identity-based politics that would seem to limit her imagination. However, focus on a single artist obscures the need for a larger discussion of the mechanisms that give some Black artists greater space, greater play, and greater recognition.

On one hand I support the right of any Black artist to create in whatever forms they want to create. But we should also be able to interrogate which artists are supported by museums, galleries, and other arms of the art establishment. Without limiting artistic freedom, I want to be free to raise critical questions about which people are elevated, and which are marginalized.

Amalia: In this case, Kara Walker did not seem prepared to discuss the enormous implications of the work she was doing, the ways in which it could be read, or why it was confirmed by a powerful white art world that lives for sex and scandal and shock. And I think being unprepared to discuss that with her Black peers was her failure as an artist. When so few of us are allowed to represent the cultures and communities we come from, each of us knows when we step out to make art we've got to be willing to take our blows.

bell: Right. When Carrie Mae Weems's work was exhibited in a New York City museum, one of the photographs included a caption which read, "Mirror, mirror on the wall. Who's the fairest of them all? Not you, Black bitch." When the Black museum guards let her know that they were troubled and felt degraded by that image, she didn't say, "I don't want to talk about it. I'm above talking about it with you." She responded to their concerns, and made these critical questions part of her creative process.

Amalia: Right.

bell: Carrie Mae Weems did not eschew the issue of accountability, because it is only in the grossest sense of individual liberalism that any artist of any race could dismiss issues of accountability. After all, we all create for an audience, and if you are not willing to consider your audience in any way, why be an artist? If you already have all those images in your head, why put them out there unless you're willing to have some kind of engagement with the world?

Amalia: Art is inherently a social practice. It's a social act, and it's embedded in one's relationship to a larger world. When you were talking about the disengagement of Black art from a political praxis, I was comparing that to the state of Chicano art—and by extension, Latino art. When Chicanos make culturally based art, it doesn't make it into the museums or galleries because it is seen as ethnically chauvinistic, provincial, or limited. Carmen Lomas Garza's cultural narratives are meaningful to people even in urban settings, but they're seen as a sort of outsider art or folk art. Somehow much of our work is constructed this way, despite the fact that we were founders in the building of the US, especially the Southwest and the West. We are still rendered almost antithetical to the larger art world.

For example, when our students visit the slide archives at Berkeley and find no Chicana or Chicano artists, they ask, "Why isn't this artist catalogued?" The response is, "Oh, well she's not a *contemporary* artist." The systems that assign the value and worth of art have determined that self-identified Chicano or Chicana artists are not contemporary artists—instead, they are folk artists or out-sider artists. This is racism, plain and simple. If you are a Chicana artist, or an artist of color, and you deal with memory, grief, love, loss, hope, home, or land, you are seen somehow as working in the illogic—it is simply not acceptable in the art world. Instead, these themes and ideas are seen as nostalgic, self-serving, and lacking the irony so prevalent in contemporary art. And it's a struggle even for artists like me, who have made work for more than thirty years—I still have to explain that what I do has relevance as a contemporary form.

bell: Also, I think that people of color have not produced enough critical analysis which explore our art practices in ways that highlight complexity. So while it is absolutely vital that we work within existing institutions, we need to create more alter-native spaces. We need institutions that are built on progressive platforms, like Intersection in San Francisco.

Amalia: We started to do it with galleries and museums.

bell: And yet there are very few progressive Black and Latino arts institutions in the United States. We are fortunate to have an institution like the Studio Museum of Harlem, but we need many more places like it. If we created progressive people of color-centered institutions, schools, museums, and think tanks in the United States that were outstanding, cool, and self-determin-ing, everybody would want to visit and use them. They would be places where fun, style, and liberatory passions could be found.

Progressives of all colors need to speak back to the con-servative uses of multiculturalism. We have to simply recognize that a radical multiculturalism has never taken root in our cultural economy, and that we are still in the process of creating theories of this radical multiculturalism. Hopefully, as the theory is created, the praxis will emerge—a union of critical thinking and critical action.

HOME

Amalia: Chicanos are people of the Americas who have been occupied twice—first by the Spanish, then by the Anglos. Therefore, when we talk about homeland, it's often tied to our rights to be in this place at this time, and to understand our own origins.

The annexation which took place after the Mexican-American War in 1848 granted us our rights to cultural citizenship, to our language, and to free transit across the California-Mexico border through the Treaty of Guadalupe Hidalgo. Yet ten years after the treaty was signed, the US government failed to provide protections, and people were effectively encapsulated and internally colonized. The Californios people lost their land in courts that quickly switched to English, a language they did not speak. Other treaties were ignored, and these people quickly found themselves at the bottom of the socioeconomic ladder. Our lives, and our resistance, has been tied to that land ever since. As a result, many of us across the Southwest mark our beginnings as a Chicano people from 1848.

Indeed, for many of us, the imposition of a border created a rupture that has never truly healed. It's almost like having a phantom limb—even though it's been removed, we share the memory of this limb, and feel its sensation. But our relationship across the Mexican border is not simply a relationship of division, separation, and loss, it is also one of continual transition. Many of us crisscross the border repeatedly and create a sense of home

somewhere between Mexico and the US, and artists like Guillermo
Gómez-Peña and David Avalos have created important work on
this theme. This helps Chicanos to talk about these simultaneous
senses of belonging and disruption.

Another important action Chicana/os can take is to reclaim
and dislocate "the border" from white critical theory, which has
constructed it as a space of difference and alterity, and reinscribe
it as a site of social agency that is connected with our rights to the
land and our spiritual wholeness.

bell: For both of us, home is a site where oppressed and
disenfranchised people restore their spirits, and continue the process of self-recovery. It is no accident that antiracist social justice
movements in the US began in the home, not the public space.
Home offered protection, so Black people in the South met in
their homes to try to figure out how to resist slavery, violence, and
Jim Crow. The contemporary feminist movement also began in
the home, with small groups of radical women doing the work of
consciousness-raising.

If you study the slave narratives and other artifacts from
slavery, home is an imaginary place. Given the conditions, slaves
had to rapidly refashion among themselves the idea of home,
since every place they stay might be temporary. Not surprisingly,
freedom in slave narratives is always connected to an ability and
capacity to create independent homes, instead of merely caring
for the homes of white people. But once the slaves were indeed
freed, most Blacks still didn't have their own independent homes.
Landowners, often their former masters, allowed them to occupy
spaces *only* so they would be used as cheap labor to work the land
again, through sharecropping, a system which was a mere step
above slavery.

So now the era of the manumitted slave/migrant worker
begins, and they are essentially nomads, constantly making and
remaking home. Growing up in the South, we were told stories
about the way Black folks came out of slavery longing for land,
confident that if they had it, they could survive. Remarkably, we
survived without it. And just like the dispossessed Chicano/as and

indigenous peoples in California you've described, these people were artisans of the earth—they knew how to make things grow. My grandmother made soap, butter, raised the animals that were then slaughtered to feed the family, made quilts out of the scraps and hand-me-downs, grew the food, had her chickens for eggs, made her wine from the grapes from our grape arbor. She had a very strong sense of economic self-sufficiency that Black people needed to survive in the agrarian South, where white supremacy limited choices.

Another way Black people resisted assimilation into the dominating culture was by reaffirming their relationships with the earth. In Buddhism the phrase is often used, "The earth is my witness." That's how many African Americans interpreted their sojourns in the agrarian South. It's crucial to remember that before the early 1900s, the vast majority of Black people lived in the agrarian South, and like Chicano/as, our historical relationship to the land was a relationship of union, husbandry, and caretaking. Black people were also quite selective about how to do this after slavery. For example, no one wanted to farm cotton for a very long time after emancipation, in spite of the fact that it might have been economically beneficial.

In *The Bluest Eye*, Toni Morrison writes that in the South, in spite of poverty, Black people can always have a relationship to the land. She describes the sensuality of nature. The color of blackberries. And I remember squeezing wild honeysuckle and smelling that perfume on my hand as a child. Morrison says all of hands-on experience of being one with nature created a culture of belonging, an eros in everyday life that is cut off as Blacks migrate to northern cities. Most importantly, in the North there was no contact with a natural world to serve as a constant reminder that white people were not all-powerful.

Daddy Jerry, my paternal grandfather, was so fond of laughing at the fact that white men could not control the sun, the rain, or make those crops grow. He knew that ultimately we could only be humble in the knowledge that nature is always beyond human will. In *Their Eyes Were Watching God*, Hurston shows this quite graphically. The hurricane comes as a reminder of God, and of what she evokes as divine spirit that shows again and again that the workings of humans are always limited.

Amalia: I think those of us raised in the laboring classes, especially in agricultural families, grew up near rural settings and are close to nature. The earliest memories I have as a child are after my father had stopped working as a migrant worker, and was employed as a ranch hand. We lived on a small ranch in the Santa Clara Valley, way before anyone had heard of "Silicon Valley." I remember picking cotton near Fresno as a child—our family shared labor, and many of my experiences with the land were communal. The first smells I recall are the smell of the earth, and the smell of the pitch pots, where the smoke goes out to keep the insects away from the trees.

But I also recognize that the migratory life has come at a high cost to many Mexican families. For example, we often bear the brunt of the enormous health risks posed by pesticides in the fields. Salinas Valley is called "salad bowl of the world," but we see pesticides such as Methlbromide being injected into the ground. Young people have protested that practice by making murals called the *fruita del Diablo*, or the fruit of the devil, which is what the Mexicans called the strawberry.

In my own teaching, I've worked with the first children of farmworkers to attend college. When they talk in class about their experiences, they often speak of the loss of their relationships with their fathers, because their fathers came here to work first and build a foothold to finally bring them from Mexico. This usually took years, and by the time they arrived, many of them no longer knew their fathers. Over time, generations of Mexican families were separated and divided by the border, creating Mexican ghost towns filled with women, children, and the aged waiting. One young woman talked about being three or four years old and playing near her house. A man walked up the driveway moving toward her, and as he got closer she became frightened and ran toward the house. When he tried to touch her, she screamed for her mother. Her mother came out and told her this is her father. At first, she didn't believe it—in her imagination, her father was the mythic man who has been working in the US making money for them, not a stranger in her yard.

Speaking about the men in our families, I liked how you described your grandfather's relationship with the land—the fact that he saw how the white man could not control the wind, nor the rain. Many African Americans drew on this knowledge for strength. I think Chicana/os have that same sense of this spiritual relationship. For example, many of the healing cures we use in our spiritual practices come from our understanding of the land. When we are children, our grandmothers go outside and pick the mint and make it into a tea when our stomachs are sick. Sage is grown and dried to be incense for the practice at our altars. We know there are many things in the landscape that are sacred, and many artists have struggled to capture them. Sometimes, in our art we have sought to document our labor, our work, and our worth, while claiming a spiritual tradition that can exist only in that geography.

bell: Mexican American culture shares this with Native American and African American culture: this sense of spiritual connection with nature as a meeting place, a point of solidarity for these groups. Historically, Blacks and Indians in the US have been willing to journey to places in nature that white men did not occupy because they were afraid of getting tuberculosis or malaria.

In her film *Daughters of the Dust*, set in the Sea Islands off the coast of North Carolina, Julie Dash depicts an African American woman and the Native American man who meet and forge a bond through their mutual respect for the land and their powerful experiences with nature. Today, most young Black folks don't care about nature or connecting with their Native American counterparts. Most Black people know very little about the Black folk in the South who cared deeply for the earth. Much of African American literature from the 1920s to the 1960s has focused on northern and industrialized Black folks who shame the country folk who have a relationship to the earth. In many of these works, northern relatives view their southern kin with contempt. They are making money at the factory, and Black farmers are working twenty-hour days, but still have no money to show for it. Yet agrarian Black folks experienced a quality of life that may have been more life-sustaining and spiritually uplifting than their northern counterparts.

In *Call to Home*, Carol Stack, an anthropologist, observes the migration of northern Blacks back to the South in the last twenty years or so. Many have left better-paying jobs to restore broken relationships with their ancestral homes. I understand this phenomenon firsthand, as I have migrated back to the Kentucky hills to smell the smells of my childhood, to watch the reeds and the marshes, and be with nature. I don't want whiteness to frame my relationship to the earth.

Amalia: The movement of Black sharecroppers in the nineteenth century and their shift away from an agrarian economy during the Depression era seems especially relevant today. As the nation has experienced cycles of recession and depression, communities of color are always at the mercy of government policies. During the Depression, Mexican laborers were aggressively scapegoated, and as a young person I heard stories about my uncle being repatriated during the 1930s. Sound familiar? And it took me years to excavate and connect other relatives' stories of traveling on Southern Pacific trains that deported Mexicans to Mexico to live and work. Not surprisingly, negotiations regarding these deportations between the US and Mexico had never been finalized, so people were repatriated to a hostile and unfriendly country. As a result, they were given land off the islands near mosquitoes and swamps. Sometimes they were driven out.

Along with the stories of repatriation, I also learned of the struggle in the fields. The people who came in the wave of immigration in the 1920s became the leaders in the fields by the 1930s. Emma Tenayuca, Louisa Moreno, and Josefina Bright—these women stood their ground in the cotton camps in the San Joaquin Valley, and were the first to be sent to Mexico by the US. In large part, this repatriation disposed of unruly Mexicans who were causing problems for agribusiness, and made way for poor whites to be exploited in the dust bowls of the 1930s.

Not surprisingly, these histories of migrating and trans-migrating the border at the behest of corporate and government interests are being reenacted. Today, the major crises we face include NAFTA, the development of the *maquiladoras*, and the continuing slaughter of hundreds of poor Mexican women near El Paso, Texas, and Juarez, Mexico.

Given these pressures, it's not surprising that Chicano activists and artists are tapping into the myth of Aztlán again—we drew on it in the 1960s. The Aztlán was located in Northern Mexico, the home of the herons, and became a part of our collective story about the journey to the North, and the founding of Tenochtitlino (Mexico City). This myth shows how we share a porous geopolitical identity, provides a sense of belonging for us, and connects us to our spiritual homeland. This story also highlights our rights to this land, which comprised more than half of the former Mexican Empire.

bell: I'm guessing that for most Black people, the "border" means the US-Mexican boundary, rising state violence, minutemen, and an assortment of economic and immigration issues writ large. But it might also mean the gap between their experiences and those of their now-distant African relatives. Since the 1960s, many Black folks have attempted to heal this rift by visiting the continent and becoming educated about African history, customs, and rituals.

Some African Americans construct Africa as "primal homeland" in very Utopian and nostalgic terms. This impulse is not surprising, because for many, many years, African Americans were taught—in a white, supremacist educational system—that we had no concrete relationship to Africa. On top of the miseducation, Africa is rarely covered in mainstream media, and it is also expensive to get there, so it's been quite difficult for most African Americans to forge a genuine relationship with their homeland. The Black Arts and Black Power Movements in the 1960s changed this somewhat, and then the television show *Roots* showed how one man had traced his genealogy back to a specific African village culture. At this point, Black people in the mainstream began to highlight and celebrate more of the retentions that linked them by name and oral history to Africa. For instance, in the late nineteenth century and early twentieth century, you could find little shacks in the South that were painted with bright colors, with yard shrines, and incredible gardens. Folks would sit on the little porches of shotgun houses and meet and greet, display their creativity, share music and stories, with each act revealing African cultural retentions. Significantly, art historians have been at the forefront of documenting these cultural retentions.

But as poor folks moved into urban areas, many settled in public housing, and this architecture was alienating. There was no place to visit with neighbors, and housing projects were often built on the borders of the town or city, so they were not a part of the actual community. Public housing undermined African American communities because it separated folks, creating class hierarchies. The infiltration of drugs into Black communities—in cities and in rural areas—brought the threat of genocide and the ruthless "do anything for money" ethic that destroys community and home.

Amalia: Within Chicano communities, we share that same struggle around addiction. And the development of gangs came out of much earlier practices of finding home, such as community federations that were cultural and also offered protection and insurance. Later, they were converted into the housing projects like White Fence and Maravilla. White Fence was identified in southern California with people who came from particular regions in Mexico, like Pachuca. And sometimes people who emigrated together formed groups, and eventually the gangs became part of a larger conflict between Norteanos (from northern Mexico) and Sureños (from Southern Mexico).

All of these connections and conflicts are invisible to people outside of the culture. These youth are simply identifiable by their clothing and their dress. Now there are lists of young people who cannot be seen congregating together, and the police have intervened so aggressively that there are specific locations where people are not allowed to stand or stop. When you speak of the relationships between addiction and criminalization and hegemony and surveillance, a lot of it starts in so-called public housing.

MEMORY

Amalia: Walter Benjamin writes that the contract between the living and the dead can never be settled cheaply. In other words, we have a duty to remember our ancestors. Some Chicano artists see memory as more than a private enterprise. Instead, it is collective and public, and it can be used to historicize. This is crucial for Chicano/as because our collective memory has been suppressed by educational institutions and the mass media. As a result, much of the communal work we have done is to inspire people to recall stories, narratives, and songs. This kind of work also positions our community to demand accountability from public institutions, like museums and granting agencies. Consequently, some institutional practices have supported the work of contemporary artists who are exploring with memory and language.

Yet contemporary cultural criticism of art, film, literature, and autobiography erases the work that Latinos and Blacks have done around memory. It is almost as if we never curated exhibits which drew on these themes, like "Ceremony of Memory," or wrote texts which discuss how memory is used in resistance. Yet as I look back on the 1980s and 1990s, our work with memory stimulated activities in our communities, and provided a tremendous organizing strategy.

bell: Definitely. For Blacks, Chicano/as, and Native Americans, memory allows us to resist and to heal: we know ourselves through the act of remembering. When we lose sight of who we are, when we lose touch, when we lose our minds, we find ourselves through remembering, through talking cures, which are reenactments of remembering. And memory becomes a thread that can bend, bind, and gather broken bits and pieces of ourselves.

Movements for self-determination among people of color have usually foregrounded the reclaiming of our histories, which lays the groundwork for building healthy self-esteem. However, it still is a radical and insurgent political gesture to return to the work of someone like Ivan Van Sertima, who documented the presence of Africans in the new world before Columbus. Van Sertima's work does not only allow us to discover something "positive" about Black folks, it also highlights the fact that Native Americans and Africans met, and were bound by cultural exchange, not domination. Of course, we know that the ethos of domination has tried to normalize conquest, and to make conflict and struggle for control inevitable and natural when two different groups meet.

Yet when we pay attention to the Africans who came here before Columbus and who were engaged with Native American culture, we see an alternative model, one that highlights partnership and mutual respect. Despite the abundance they found here, the Africans who arrived before Columbus wanted to go home, and return to their familiar languages, customs, and culture. This counterhegemonic moment has been suppressed by white supremacist imperialism, because their behavior showed that partnerships could be formed outside of dominating culture.

Amalia: One of the most hopeful recent developments in Mexico is the work of some activists to push for public recognition of our long-standing relationship with African people. It's called the *Terca Ruiz*, or the Third Root, and they established it to expand the history of Mexico. It's ironic that as various Chicano intellectuals and activists are pursuing this rich African legacy, the Mexican government puts out postage stamps with racist images on them! Mexico, like the United States, has usually suppressed this kind of history, but this project is an indication that some are willing to examine the country's complexity. As Chicano/as, it is one part of our long struggle to name ourselves and name where we come from.

After all, Chicano/as have been accused of being a people really without a history, as though all of us were immigrants. We're "new" to this country every decade, every century we appear in the United States—and then, we're new again. So it is essential for us to recover our collective memory. We must talk about what was lost through the incursion of the border, through the separation and loss of the multitudes, and remember the millions killed through violence, disease, and brutal labor conditions in the so-called ages of discovery in Mexico.

During this genocidal era, this region was seen as an empty paradise and an uncivilized space waiting to be tamed. People came with their own memories from the old world, and they renamed the plants, the animals, and the places to suit themselves and to assuage their own memory and loss as invaders who had come this great distance. And they sought to perpetuate the belief that we had no memory. I recall that in one of the journals kept during the fall of Tenochtitlan (Mexico City), *La Noche Triste*, or the Sad Night, a Meso-American writer says, "we have beat our heads against the walls. They are splattered with brains, the waters run with blood. We taste the brine of our own loss. Not even our greatest warriors can protect us. Our spears are broken. Our city is lost. Our inheritance is gone." These words capture the enormity of the loss, a loss only redeemed by our willingness to remember and witness.

bell: And as people of color and women utilize memory as a site of resistance, white hegemony responds, "Why all of this confession, why all this testimony?" But when we are engaged in this psychological, archaeological dig—when we rediscover not just the facts of history, but the psychohistory—we learn about our ancestors in a different way. For example, when we discover that slave women didn't just think about killing their children to prevent them from being enslaved, they did it, as Toni Morrison documents in *Beloved*, we have a new and very complex vision of Black female resistance.

For example, in Spike Lee's documentary, *Four Little Girls*, he jolts us from any belief that racism is not still alive. He challenges people who say, "If you're not able to get ahead, it's your problem," and who wish to maintain that there is no white supremacist conspiracy and no daily assaults by white supremacy. What he skillfully reveals is a systemic white supremacy that is not just institutional, but is about everyday silences and collusion. We see a white father teaching his son not to lie, but at the same time lying to his son about what really happened. We see that same white boy, now a man, reflecting back on his past and confronting the ways this lying was traumatic. We see the sister of one of the dead girls, who was forced by a policeman to identify the decapitated body of her sister, suffering from mental illness as a consequence.

It is one of the first times that we can witness the impact of racial terrorism and post-traumatic stress on the psyches of African Americans. In that documentary, Spike Lee shows us the intertwinings of psychohistory—the historical facts and their impact on our emotional world. He shows us how facts were distorted—at the very time that white people were telling Black folks they were our friends, they were also beheading us. They maintained, "We don't know who would do this." When all along, many white people knew exactly who was doing it.

The first time I saw *Four Little Girls* was in the company of a huge body of schoolchildren. They learned that children were very much a part of the social justice and antiracist movements. We all need to be reminded that resistance doesn't simply involve adults; it is also about children and youth culture. When we use memory as a tool to reclaim lost and stolen histories, it is always in the interest of our freedom and self-determination.

Amalia: And I would say that even beyond our own capacity to individually remember, or the capacity of a community to sustain memory, there is actually a way that nature itself remembers. I have a friend, Ismael Frigerio, the Chilean artist, who created a project called *Nature: The Never Ending Witness*. It springs from work he did in Chile during the time of the *desaparecidos*, or the "disappeared ones." In Chile, like in other places in Latin America, the memory of mothers, who have paraded in squares and held up images of their lost children, has brought the murderous practices of dictatorships to public consciousness. In this project, he documents the discovery of bodies of the disappeared. They were pushed from airplanes and dropped into the northern deserts of Chile, with the expectation that no one would ever find them. But pilgrims who go on spiritual journeys and walk there did find these bodies, and little by little their reports reached people. Over time, it became known that the landscape was filled with marks of death and destruction.

Nature also plays a different role in our practice of remembering. For example, we leave flowers and fruit for the dead, this is how we mark our tragedies. And events which haunt a family—the death of a young man in war, the death of a newborn child—are articulated in the home altar, and then sometimes in prayers, and always in storytelling. Every family has stories, and altar records the struggles and losses, as well as instances of resistance and triumph.

bell: I think it's difficult for many people who lack critical awareness to understand how memory serves as a resource for resistance and for spiritual healing. I often share the way positively remembering the Black men in my family counters the daily bombardments of negative representations generated by mainstream white supremacist culture. I write in *Bone Black* about my grandfather that "his smells fill my nostrils with the scent of happiness. With him all the broken bits and pieces of my heart come together again." It's oppositional to present real, lived experiences of loving and caring Black men when we are daily assaulted by images of them as brutal, dehumanized, and incapable of tenderness and care. These hateful images are brought to us largely through the machinations of a white conservative-dominated mass media which draws on criminality, gangster rap, and misogynist hip-hop for its representations. In some ways, the more virulent forms of gangster rap are assaults on the collective memory of Black people, because music has been a primary site of resistance in African

American life. Singers like Otis Redding, Jackie Wilson, and Ray Charles gave us music that revealed emotional depth. Fortunately, we see a counterhegemonic music coming forth, with the positive music of people like Lauryn Hill, Mos Def, Talib Kweli, Jean Grae, Common, India Arie, and Jill Scott. Music can be a powerful healing force, partially through its evocation of memories.

When we see memory as a gift that we can consciously use to enhance life and live more fully, we can recognize that our ability to remember is at risk in a culture where only the present moment matters. For instance, instead of sitting down and talking with their grandmothers and grandfathers, young people are deeply enmeshed in passive consumer culture. I vividly remember the joy that I felt going to my grandmother Baba's house. My grandmother could not read or write, but I could engage her in lively conversations about the past and I wanted to hear her stories. When we are young, we don't just want to hear the story once—we want to hear it over and over and over again. So I would say to my grandmother, tell me the story about such-and-such, until it was imprinted in my heart's memory. Many people, young and old, have asked me how I remembered the details that are in *Bone Black* and *Wounds of Passion*. I tell them that I spent hours and hours sitting and talking with my grandparents, and many of them cannot relate to that.

You and I agree that we have to value conversation and storytelling, because our memories and histories are shared and kept alive through these practices. If people of color buy into a culture that circumvents our dialogues with one another, especially our intergenerational dialogues, we do profoundly limit our capacity to remember. Memories are made, as conscious and unconscious resources, and they are gifts that we must be ready and willing to receive.

I very much like the quote by filmmaker Luis Buñuel, when he wisely acknowledges that you have to begin to lose your memory—if only in bits and pieces—to realize that memory is what makes our lives. Life without memory is no life at all. Our memory is our coherence, our reason, our feeling, even our actions.

Amalia: When you talk about the importance of your grandmother to your life and work, I remember how my father and his brothers shared stories about my grandmother. They told us that she worked in migrant camps and stood her own against people who would denigrate her, or try to prevent her from feeding and clothing her children. She was known to have hurtled people through windows if they treated her badly! And she visited *curanderas* to find cures to keep them well in difficult periods. Their stories from the migrant camps—how they moved from place to place with their belongings loaded in trucks, searching for places to work—are expressions of the most extreme and acute suffering *and* of how they overcame it. So those memories were instructive to me—they were lessons about resiliency.

Carmen Lomas Garzas's paintings, particularly the ones that deal with migrant life, such as *Abuelitos Piscando Nopalites* (the grandparents picking cactus), or the works featuring childhood piñata parties, are visual stories that serve as alternative chronicles of life for people whose stories have never been celebrated or "officialized." I've been in museums where I've seen parents take their children up to those paintings and very carefully explain to the child every element in the painting so that they won't forget that way of life. Thankfully, these images have been catalogued in books, which have sold in the hundreds of thousands in California, Texas, and New Mexico alone.

The muralist Judith Baca has been able to bring enormous visual power to her Los Angeles project on the *Great Wall*. Baca invites storytellers to talk about the Japanese internment camps; the forced relocation of Chavez Ravine, a thriving Mexican American community in LA, in 1949; the dust bowl farmers who moved to the west coast during the Depression era; or stories about the Civil Rights Movement. The *Great Wall* is the largest mural in the world—it runs through a cemented Los Angeles river, and has allowed visitors to tap into suppressed or censored collective memories. Sometimes the people telling these stories are young people, who heard them from their elders.

Earlier, we talked about liberation pedagogy. If we make classroom spaces where young people can offer testimonials and witness the history of their own families and not face punishment or censorship, then the space truly becomes democratic. If this happened, personal narratives could provide tools for us to learn.

bell: And the process of becoming a subject, of owning one's story, is necessary for self-recovery, for the building of self-esteem. The African Burial Grounds in New York City is now a historical site, marked by public art. The site is not only a reminder of the presence of African-descended people in the "new world," but it has forced people to recognize our labor and our role in the development of advanced capitalism.

But we also have to remember that an overwhelming and countervailing impulse is to look away. Several years ago, California held reparations hearings for the Japanese who were interned in relocation camps here. These hearings did not command the global media attention they should have, as the camps were infamous sites of racial terrorism, not just prejudice. I was deeply moved as I listened to these Japanese people talk about their sense of shame, and their desires never to speak of this past.

But people of color desperately need a practice of remembering that is not nostalgic, which allows for these kinds of intervention to occur. For instance, we can acknowledge the Black Panther Party's marvelous interventions as soldiers for self-determination, while also remembering the ways the organization was sexist, misogynist, and self-hating. Simply put, we need to end selective remembering. Some Afrocentric thinking can be plagued by this kind of blindness, as Africa is constructed as a place where only kings and queens lived. Oftentimes I say to people, "What about the slaves who built the pyramids. Do we disidentify with them?"

If we engage in these practices of forgetfulness, as in the dominating culture, we will likely invent narratives where we are conquerors. Instead of fantasies, we need to work out genuine relationships of mutuality. If we stay in the nostalgic framework, it's paralyzing.

Amalia: You've talked about how an Afrocentric positivism creates the fictive history of an idealized African and of an idealized Africa. In the early years of the Chicano movement, many of us were invested in an idealized Mexico because we were desperate for images of beauty and power that would sustain us, and our real histories and stories had been suppressed. In the early 1980s, I remember attending two exhibitions with other activists and artists. One of them was a series of paintings by a famous Mexican painter called Helguera who had trained in Spain. He'd been hired by a tobacco company to travel throughout Mexico and capture "Mexican culture." On display, there were a *vaquero*, a *charro* on horseback, a woman at the altar praying at a baptismal and other images from history—including Malinalli, the Native American woman who was the companion of Cortes. People like Dolores del Río and Jorje Negrete—elite Euro-Mexicans who were movies stars in Mexico's cinematic age, the 1930s and 1940s—were the faces of indigenous people in the paintings!

Across town at the Galería de la Raza was another exhibition called *Cactus Hearts and Barbed Wire Dreams*, an exhibition by Yolanda López. She presented her collection of Mexican stereotypic imagery—including Taco Bell toys and 1930s salt and pepper shakers of sleeping Mexicans. Here were the two poles: the hyperidealism and falseness of a fictive Mexico, and hateful, ugly, and stereotypic images of Mexico manufactured for consumption in the US. As Chicanos, I think we had been so demeaned and offended by negative stereotypes that we rushed headlong into the embrace of a hyperidealistic Mexico. It wasn't the Mexico our parents left in revolution or in poverty.

bell: Our commitment to healing is predicated on our responsibility to be honest about the past, and tell the truth even if what we must share is negative or ugly. Within African American communities, we have also worked to suppress some of our memories, particularly those memories that show us in a bad light. For instance, we don't often discuss the historical impact of internalized racism in our everyday lives or the way acceptance of the vicious color caste system has created profound emotional violence and damage. Our memories of incest and domestic violence are also censored. To fight the revolution, we have to contend with these histories. We have to excavate, look, and talk about it all. While much of our resistance history has been suppressed by white hegemony, African Americans are also collectively involved in creating false images. Only recently have African American progressives begun to tell full and complex stories, without concern for how those stories will be perceived by white and Black folks.

Amalia: When you were talking about the caste system, I was thinking about how Mexicans still have to come to terms with this in our own culture. We spoke earlier about the *castas* paintings that were made during the eighteenth and nineteenth centuries in Mexico. The Spanish, establishing a form of racial apartheid, delineate the fifty-three categories of racial mixtures between Africans, Indians, and the Spanish. And they have names, like *teinte en el aire*, which means stain in the air; and *salta atras*, which means jump back; or *mulatto*, a word that comes from mula, the unnatural mating between the horse and the donkey. "Sambo" is now a racial epithet in the US, but it was first used as one of the fifty-three racial categories in the *castas* paintings.

This shared language and imagery recalls the ugly history of colonization. But the caste paintings also help us understand that we were together in our suffering, abuse, and genocide of that era. Our lives and races and histories are still mixed together, and if we examine this visual and social history, we might find a way to understand present struggles. One of the most radical paintings shows a Spanish woman and an African woman in identical dress standing side by side, surrounded by the fruits of paradise. On the surface, the caste painting is not about the taxonomy of those women, it is about the taxonomy of the fruit and the fauna. But these women challenged the limitations placed on their dress and on their relationships. Learning how indigenous and African-descended people faced oppression, and even outwitted a system of social apartheid, gives us inspiration even now. We, as people of color, are linked to one another.

ALTARS

bell: Amalia, your art has given the power of the altar—particularly as an icon in Mexican American life—much greater visibility in the US.

Amalia: I have played a big part in a movement, but of course it's been a collective effort, so I haven't been alone. There are others, including my mentor, Yolanda Garfias Woo, Ralph Maradiaga, and Carmen Lomas Garza. People have often asked why I have chosen to do this kind of work, particularly in light of the contemporary art world's animosity toward religiosity and spirituality. Some people have chastised me for sustaining a practice that they see as provincial, folkloric, or self-servingly ethnic. But I've always said that my relationship to altars and creativity precedes my time in art school; it goes back to my childhood.

My mother was orphaned young and lived in a convent for part of her childhood, so she was very familiar with Catholic altars. And my paternal grandmother, Mariana Escobedo Mesa, came from Mexico during the revolution in 1916. This move was a tremendous and traumatic rupture in her life, but one way she was able to heal herself and maintain the centrality of the home was through her home altar. She kept it in her bedroom atop her dresser. Every family has their favorite saints, and my grandmother, who I believe was mixed-race, loved St. Martin de Porros because he was dark skinned.

So I grew up around the home altar, the church altar, the yard shrines or *capillas*, the little chapels that my godmother kept. And from an early age, I was aware that altars mediate our relationships with the divine and the sacred within our homes. Also, most people don't recognize that the home altar is a counterpoint to church patriarchy, because home altars are presided over by a female figure in the family, like my grandmother and my mother. The church has its patriarchy of priests, but families often have a matriarchal spirituality.

Early exposures to home altars and yard shrines inspired many Chicanos to create art that would serve the community during in the 1960s and 1970s. And two tropes helped us organize their ideas: resistance and affirmation. Resistance art critiqued colonial practices, hegemony, white racism. Affirmation-centered art helped us reclaim practices that made us unique as a people, and which had sustained our culture in hostile environments, including the traditions of the home altar. So in the early days, I remember going home and asking my family many questions about my grandmother's altar.

Many of us were first- and second-generation Mexicans in the US, so we actively engaged in what I called "cultural reclamation." My compadre Tomas Ybarra Frausto coined the phrase "nutrient sources" to refer to community practices which had nourished us. This included the making and keeping of the altars, maintaining respect for the dead and the Days of the Dead traditions, and making and keeping of yard shrines that were sometimes converted into political displays. People began by putting saints or virgins in them, but later people began to imbed with them other things, like mosaics of broken plates, Christmas lights, even waterfalls.

I think that one of the most salient aspects of the altar is the centrality of the icon itself, whether the Virgin of Guadalupe, a transformative figure that connects the Tonantzins, or the Mother Goddesses, or the Santo Niño de Atoche, the "little child that journeys." Every altar has an iconography, and each seeks to bring together the living and the dead. These are the things that you learn right away when you start doing them in public.

I remember doing our first Day of the Dead *ofrendos* at the Galería de la Raza, which involved making temporary and ephemeral offerings to the dead, instead of the permanent and ongoing offering made at the altar. I was purposefully fusing the two. I placed the image of my sister with my grandmother, and I added my own face mask, and immediately the old women in the community came in to tell us that this was very bad luck and very dangerous. In an offering to the dead, you never include an image of the living. They could not accept that I was merging two traditions—the permanent, ongoing record of the family in the altar and the temporary, ephemeral practice of the offerings for the dead. For them, they were two separate things.

I continued with the practice and adapted and innovated on it, and as I worked through this form, it became clear why altars have been sustaining to families—they're a form of memory-making and history-making, and they accrue. They're desirable because they have layers, so that at any moment you see an altar you understand the complexity and endurance of your family. You will see the medals from your uncle who died in the war, you will see your own baby booties, you will see the dried flowers from your cousin's wedding, you will see the images of your mother and father as a young bride and groom, you will see the face of your great-grandfather, and you will see the image of the newborn child, because they are all in a cosmology of the family centered in memory that is linked to the present. The altar is sacred because it protects the family, and it protects the belongings of the family. For instance, all the important family papers are there—whether they are the tax papers, baptismal records, marriage licenses, or insurance papers, things of value are kept in the space under the altar.

Many people have talked about it as a form of *rasquachismo*, or as we say in the Chicano community, "making the most from the least." Yard shrines, for example, can be made out of broken plates, old marbles, cut-up Clorox bottles—there is nothing beneath your consideration when you are elaborating these things, they have their own logic. I've always been mystified when people call home altars "catches," because they really are not. They're not

mass produced or coming from a dominant society that identifies them as valuable. They're often handmade, and have elements
which reflect the ingenuity of the family members themselves.
And there are always signs of the natural, signs of the indigenous
within those altars. They serve as a sacred space, and as a place
where women have power.

bell: Like Mexican Americans, Black folks in the South
often constructed altars, in spite of patriarchal Christianity's influence, which discouraged people from having altars in their homes.
Within the fundamentalist Christian church, the altar always
played an important role. As a girl, I sang the song called "Is Your
All on the Altar of Sacrifice Laid?" The altar was the place you
could bring your burdens, lay them down, and be restored.

I've written about spaces in the African American southern home that are shrines made up of photographs and mementos.
As a child, I certainly was awed when I stood before these shrines
to our ancestors, these shrines that told our family narratives. In
childhood, we would learn about the dead from looking at these
walls of photographs.

As a child, there was a peculiar way that I held my hands
and I remember looking at images of my Aunt Hettie Lou, who
died young. I saw that she held her hands in similar ways. This was
an awesome revelation. These shrines communicated psychohistory of a genealogy of the soul and graphically showed how traits,
interests, beliefs are passed down. And as with Mexican American
women, shrine-making offers a spiritual and creative practice
to African Americans that is beyond the confines of patriarchy.
Making altars was a way to worship, to be restored, and to show
devotion.

Amalia: *Curanderismo*, or that curing worldview and healing
practice, is also the same intermediary space that the home altar
occupies as a sacred practice, where the individual communicates
through this intermediary space with the divine, where the ce-
lestial is always present in the everyday lives of people, so that
home altars are accepted in many families. And Chicano artists

and cultural workers see the narrative tradition embodied by the home altar, and use it in forms like installations and ritual practices, which build communities.

bell: In her scholarship on Haitian voudou, Zora Neale Hurston shows how "Blackness" in the US has always been hybrid, a "composite," a mixture of customs and practices from Africa, the Caribbean, and the Americas. So prior to establishment of the church, spirituality is embodied through shrines, places in the slave's cave like hut that are private and secret: the white master could not even understand how the rocks and pieces of herb mounted constituted an altar, a place of power in the life of the powerless.

The art of enslaved Blacks, often fashioned from found objects, helped to maintain a sacred space which was fashioned to meet their needs. Long before Carl Jung wrote about the collective unconscious, African Americans were seeking concrete ways to be guided and inspired by the spirit world. Shrines and altars were tools that helped us from losing our minds in the face of such violence and brutality. They were tools that helped us resist, even in small ways, domination.

Our traditions certainly do overlap, and you can see it in the work of contemporary artists like Bettye and Allison Saar. Whether consciously or unconsciously, their work has been informed by Mexican and African American iconography and tradition. They draw on memories of yard shrines and altars, as well as the cultural hybridity at the heart of the African American experience

Amalia: Why do you think the larger society has been so attracted to these practices? I'm guessing it is a reflection of the vacuousness and the emptiness of dominant culture—people really don't have a place to grieve or mourn. Our society has a built-in way of targeting "obsolescence," of disposing of anything but the new, the innovative, the young. As a result, for example, people who lose a loved one are seen as abnormal if they actively grieve for longer than two or three months.

bell: This is a characteristic of a conquest society and of dominant culture, which is why so many public monuments in the US are merely representations of conquest, triumph, or destruction instead of something more complex and nuanced. One of the lovely aspects of the contemporary revisioning of the mission in San Juan Baptista is the beautiful statue of the Indian. There is a statue of a priest closer to the chapel, but I was drawn to this sculpture of the Native American Indian. This monument offers a very different exposure to public art, which more often than not, celebrates white cultural imperialism.

Amalia: Judy Baca often refers to that statue as the "canon in the park." It does stand out. Usually only the victor has the story to be told, the public memory is held only by those who vanquish others. And all people are hungry for some way to publicly express their own sense of loss. So, for example, after September 11, people simply felt this incredible need to grieve collectively, so they came out of their homes and built shrines, or *descansos*. Similar shrines are being created in Louisiana, to remember those people who were taken by the storm and the flooding. A *descanso* is a resting place, and it's usually a shrine on the side of the road that usually acknowledges an accident and a death or a tragedy, and you see them often in rural areas.

bell: When we talk about death, there is always that commonality, for death is the great equalizer. We are *all* journeying towards death, and it is the altar on which we surrender our differences and become one.

DAY OF THE DEAD

bell: All over the world, people of color face incredibly difficult prospects. Exploitation, poverty, oppression, and lack of access to food, clean water, and medical care means that too many of us are familiar with the process of helping someone to die, or we are prematurely facing death ourselves. For example, life expectancies for African-descended people all over the world compare poorly to European-descended people. When you look to Africa, the situation on the continent is especially devastating—in many countries, it has become exceptional to live beyond forty.

And as we've recently seen in New Orleans, South Asia, and Pakistan, after the hurricane, tsunami, and earthquakes, there is no such thing as a solely "natural" disaster with solely "natural" consequences. Being a person of color and poor tipped the scales for millions toward displacement, illness, and death, even in the wealthy US. It's impossible to talk about revolution, new ways of living, without talking about facing these realities.

Then there are those of us made physically and emotionally vulnerable by obscene wars. Three years into the "War on Terror," nearly 100,000 civilians have been killed in Iraq, and thousands more are dead in Afghanistan.

Amalia: In the face of the enormous abuse, violence, disease, and exploitation you've spoken of, one of the sources of revitalization and resistance that has existed in some cultures is a collective understanding of the relationship between the living and the dead. The Latin American community developed practices and traditions that sustained us long before the Spanish arrived and which have persisted beyond the colonial enterprise, the Anglo intervention, and the taking of territory. Many of these traditions are connected with the Day of the Dead.

The Day of the Dead is an ancient Meso American tradition honoring the dead as they passed into the afterlife. The Spanish colonials tried to subsume it under the Catholic calendar as "All Souls' Day" in early November, but some of the rituals, as well as the offerings—flowers, food, candles—remained indigenous.

In the tradition that existed before the Spanish invaded, ancestral worship of the dead was articulated through practices and in cosmology in which "Mictlan," or the Land of the Dead, was where souls pass through various stages of transformation until they reach oblivion. Particular groups of people had special places in Mictlan, such as warriors who died in battle, and mothers who died in childbirth. The indigenous traditions mandated people to remember the dead during specific seasons. When the Spanish came to colonize, they co-opted the practice, since they could find no way to exterminate it. Just as they built cathedrals on the ruins of temples they destroyed, they gathered and aggregated these traditions of ancestor worship and regard for the dead around "All Souls' Day."

As a result, our traditions have been linked to contemporary and ancient concepts around death and dying. But in the Mexican American community, the Day of the Dead still provides a space to face some of challenges you described: illness, poverty, exploitation, violence, racism, and death. During the celebration, two or three days are spent in traditional communal rituals which link the ancestors and the processional. Those moments become an intersection between the joyous celebration of the dead, and resolution and resignation to the reality of death. People set aside money to create amazing altars so they can enjoy two days of beauty.

We call the offerings that we make to the dead *ofrendos* and *altares*, and the act of remembering allows us to transcend the loss, grieving, and our fear of death. I have sometimes talked about it as a politicizing spirituality; through it, I believe we have developed skills that allow us to face the acute conditions and challenges that might decimate others. In Spanish they will say *"cada vida tiene su pena"*—every life has its burden. But I've learned how to sustain myself in the face of death and dying.

bell: In traditional African American folk culture, there was always a recognition that death is imminent, and always around. After all, one of the most segregated institutions in the United States prior to the Civil Rights Movement was the hospital. There are many, many narratives of folk dying en route to the nearest place that would take a Black person, bypassing hospital after hospital. Even so, I grew up in one of the few towns in the South that had an all-Black hospital. But it did not have many beds. So it was tacitly understood within the community that if someone had a life-threatening illness and was on the edge of death, they were not taken to the hospital—the bed must be surrendered to someone who could recover. In this situation, it was understood that folks who might survive were privileged.

Death is presented as a friend, as a comforter, and as inevitable in James Weldon Johnson's poetry. And when I was young, this recognition was essential to an organic meaning of life in the South. This stood in contrast to the white Western sense that death can be defeated and denied. In the African American experience, we have been more willing to acknowledge our powerlessness in relationship to death, and to answer the questions "How are you living your life? Will you be ready to die? Will you be able to stand and account for the life you have led?"

When Elisabeth Kübler-Ross was searching for a way to deal with the death she constantly witnessed as a doctor in Chicago, she observed a Black cleaning lady routinely entering the rooms of the dying. As this Black woman left each room, a transformation had taken place—the patients had a sense of peace and reconciliation, when before, there was only terror and anguish. Kübler-Ross confronts the Black woman and asks, "What are you doing in there?" But she won't tell her. Finally, Kübler-Ross hides behind a curtain and observes this Black woman sharing her own story of losing a child unexpectedly in life, and of death coming to her again and again. Instead of talking about it as a tragedy, the Black woman talks about death as a potential moment of awakening where one can renew one's vows to life.

Kübler-Ross built her theory of how we might die in peace informed by this profound experience. Sadly, she never gives the name of this Black woman in her writing or in her autobiographical statements, which is typical of white cultural imperialism and a competitive academic practice. And the erasure of this Black woman's name, an honor she was due, is also the denial of what has been taken from her. This was not a reciprocal process of sharing.

Stephen Levine has written many books on how people in the US cope with dying. He talks about people across class divides, not racial divides. Like so many others theorists, he writes about death and dying without ever talking about people of color. Yet all over our nation, nurses and caregivers who are less well-paid in hospitals, nursing homes, and hospices are often people of color. Nowadays, the people who do the dirty work of caring for the sick and the dying are usually people of color. And very few people are theorizing about the importance and nature of that care, something the poor, disenfranchised, and the dispossessed still are generous enough to give.

Day of the Dead rituals strike me as another example of people of color having profound insight into the living and dying process, despite being discounted and shoved into the margins of these discussions. By confronting death, we can find a space of celebration and, as you rightly state, a place of fugitive joy.

Amalia: In the same way, rituals around the Day of the Dead always incorporate humor. For instance, some of us offer candy skulls with the name of a beloved, a *calavera* claiming a love that transcends death. These practices are supported by belief systems that have sustained us for centuries. Nothing is permanent in this life; we don't own this land or this world; we are visitors like the spring grass—we've come to blossom, to bud, to wither, to dry up, and blow away.

As you can see, many of the values and beliefs that sustain the Day of the Dead fly in the face of capitalism and individualism. So, it's not surprising that many white people have distorted and disfigured the tradition. They come to us for our processionals and our gatherings, but soon enough their misunderstanding of our humor and joy turns into the carnival of Halloween, and thousands of them come in Los Angeles and in San Francisco for the processional for the moment of transformation, and they sully it. They destroy it. They make it back into the fearful caricature of their own "All Hallows."

Nonetheless, I have seen more young people at our university treasuring this form of remembrance. They especially appreciate the altars and Aztec dancers. Many young people need these practices to face life. And when you talk about the care for the dead, and I think of the traditions of vigil, and I think of people like César Chávez, who were willing to fast and risk their lives to show the spiritual core of political agency. I remember when a two-week hunger strike, led in 1993 by UCLA students who supported the establishment of a Chicana studies department, reached the twelfth day. Their parents were there praying for them, yet no one asked them to stop; they had joined a tradition of sacrifice, which is the other side of service. Our traditions around death and dying have never been solely about celebration, ceremony, mythic reconstructions, or nostalgia; they have always been tied to resistance and struggle. Fasting and vigils show respect for the service and sacrifice of others.

bell: No wonder the dominant culture cannot acknowledge these rituals of remembrance. How can they, when the US is involved in the wholesale slaughter of peoples of color all over the world, every day? How can we really talk about honoring death? Furthermore, within the rituals as you describe them, there is a constant affirmation of joy and struggle. Joy often comes in the wake of the sacrifice, so that one can answer that question as the spiritual does: "Is your all on the altar of sacrifice laid? Is your all doth the spirit control?" You can only be blessed and have peace and sweet rest when all on the altar is laid.

Amalia: This tradition of spirituality and sacrifice is also part of art's power to transform moments of struggle into a language that creates meaning and understanding. For example, I think of the piece that Puerto Rican installation artist Pepón Osorio did at the Museo del Barrio in New York, *El Velorio* (the wake).

In this work, Osorio examined what had happened in the Bronx and Spanish Harlem in the late 1980s and early 1990s. Many young men had been dying of AIDS, but their families did not celebrate their deaths because of the stigma they felt would mark them. They were already in poverty and distress, and so they quietly died and were quietly buried. No *velorio*, no wake, no celebration was prepared—their deaths were not marked by joy, food, or music.

Pepón began collecting the stories from the mothers and grandmothers of these young men, and he asked a funeral home to lend him caskets. He filled the caskets with transparent images of photographs of these young men, and he wrote on the rug and on the wall of this large room, arranged like a funeral parlor with little benches for people to sit on. He wrote the quotes and stories from these families talking about the love they had for these young men, and the sadness they felt in not acknowledging their deaths. Finally, he made each of them elaborate flower decorations, which rested like floral sprays on caskets, and on the first night only the families of these young men were invited to come.

They didn't know each other, but they formed an immediate community to have the *velorio* that they had not been able to have. And later other people came, and more and more people came, so they had to extend the exhibition—the museum had been turned into a space for mourning and memory, and this *velorio* was a wake that lasted for several months. Whether we call it spiritual art or folk art, there is clearly a capacity to translate our most difficult moments of our lives into something collective and public.

bell: You and I grew up in a time where we very rarely knew someone young who died. We are now in the midst of a culture where you hardly find a poor urban family whose members have not experienced several deaths of very young people, through violence, illness, or AIDS. Young people of color, particularly those living in cities, face death routinely.

Several years ago, I ran a writing workshop for young people in New York City. I was stunned when these ten- and eleven-year-olds wrote so much about death, loss, and grief. Because they don't live in a culture that endows each death with meaning, merely witnessing these deaths causes profound despair. How can a fifth-grader cope with so much death? Why should they have to? People of color must do the activism necessary to eliminate violence and illness in our communities, and we also must return to our remembrance rituals. We can't hide or minimize these losses from young people, or leave them with the idea that death is their fate, no matter what they do in life.

Amalia: Indeed. The traditions of the Day of the Dead, which Chicanos reclaimed for political reasons in the 1960s, are becoming a vehicle for young people to honor people lost through violence or other forms of injustice. In the last number of years, we have been working in many Latino communities with gang intervention programs in Salinas, California, such as Second Chance, to create spaces for people to publicly speak about the violence so, perhaps, something could be healed. A group of students we worked with in Salinas created a wall of remembrance where they placed the photographs of friends who had died—ten-year-olds, twelve-year-olds, fourteen-year-olds. And we continue to work with farmworkers and their families who have lost loved ones through work-related accidents or illness.

bell: Before their first encounter with dying, many of the young people I've talked with have said they believed death was not permanent. And in many cases where children have shot other children, they're surprised when the other child is not resurrected. That's how alienated we have become in our understanding of the true violence of meaningless death. So without forms of recovery and activism like the wall of remembrance, we limit our understanding of how we might fully live and how we might change concrete and material conditions, to end unnecessary deaths.

Martin Luther King and Malcolm X have always been heroic to me because both of them understood that they were going to be asked to give their all—their lives—on the altar of sacrifice. When Martin Luther King stands up and announces in that fearful, trembling voice, "I am not afraid of any man tonight. Because I have been to the mountaintop, and I have seen the promised land," he is really talking about that prescient and rare moment when you understand that you are going to die for what you believe in, and you are prepared to do so fearlessly. This is what we mean when we talk about death with integrity. Both of these men did not live to see forty. That their deaths happened in the sweetness of their lives, and yet as they approached the reality of death, they were having new and even more visionary insights about ending domination, and creating a peaceful and just world.

Despite the clouds closing in around us now—US terrorism and the torture of innocents, warmongering, the rise of imperialism, and the growing gap between rich and poor—I'm afraid we've forgotten what it means to be prepared to sacrifice in that manner. Think about the Buddhist nun who self-immolates in sadness and joy, who says, "I want so badly to let the world know about the meaning of peace that I burn myself; I give myself over." If people can't access that philosophy, we cannot build resistance. We will not be redeemed, and we will not talk with our ancestors. We see this in the Day of the Dead rituals as well. People of color who are grounded in a sense of ancestor worship are in touch with traditions that honor death and can choose to live our lives with greater vigilance. We understand that without critical vigilance, we cannot survive.

Afterword

bell: Since 9-11, we've been in the throes of a hypernationalist, hysterical moment. This tragedy allowed conservative, right-wing, white supremacist policies to be more easily pushed through, including an immoral invasion and war, the plundering of social services to support the military, and vast and lasting changes in US immigration policies. Like other people of color, Blacks and Latinos have born the brunt of these changes. But many of these fascist policies were being put in place before 9-11; that event became the catalyst for a reinscription of these things. A harsher inscription. The latest debates on immigration surely tap into this thinking.

Amalia: Certainly. And for Mexicans, draconian immigration policies go *way* back. In the 1920s, people who had been union organizers in the fields—many of them with citizenship—were deported to Mexico. Then there were the "Operation Wetback" deportations in the 1950s. There's a cycle of ambivalence with regard to Mexico on the part of the US. The US demonizes us as lazy and parasitic, sends us back, then brings us back again when our labor is needed. This has been going on for a *very* long time. What's new is the very public resistance and critique; the marches in support of immigrants rights in US cities were simply stunning.

bell: Part of the demonizing is about denial; people do not want to acknowledge that many Black people and poor white people are unwilling to do agricultural labor. Very few Black people live in my small Kentucky town, but there is a burgeoning Latino population. Many work in the tobacco and tomato fields, and it's been perplexing to see how my little "liberal" town, rooted in abolitionist history, has responded. For example, a progressive, white, feminist professor suggested that the Catholic church offer a Mass in Spanish. The conservative forces were initially quite strongly opposed. The uproar amounted to, "If they can't speak English, they should go back to their country." This is nothing but white supremacist resistance. And it comes not just from the right, but from liberals who are running scared. People are afraid of what will happen to white hegemony if we all learn Spanish. It's a question of power, and it really calls into question all of our academic theories about postcolonialism. It's not "postcolonial" at all.

Amalia: No, we're not "over" colonialism. Just think about the undocumented workers who died on 9-11; their names were never added to any lists, and their families were never given any reparation. They were only acknowledged by the Mexican Syndicatos who organized efforts to determine who they were, because before they disappeared, they worked under the table at Windows on the World or cleaning offices. This group of people simply disappeared in the ashes.

These were the people who come early to set up the restaurants, and who finish their all-night cleaning shifts early in the morning. But we weren't allowed to talk about their fates, because it could have lead to the realization that there were plausible rationales for 9-11. We couldn't tolerate that; we had to recreate it as a wholly irrational act.

bell: And so far, the most dangerous assault on American freedom bar none has been the Patriot Act, which permits the government to overturn our civil liberties. When I hear people in airports say, "I don't mind giving up certain freedoms in order to be safe," it disturbs me. So I stand up and talk to audiences about the history of fascism, and point out that this is precisely the kind of thinking that led to the Nazi Holocaust—in order to be safe, we must give up our freedoms.

Amalia: And as we see our freedoms and our rights to privacy dissolve, our government is off insisting on democracy in parts of the world where the model isn't necessarily relevant.

bell: It's like Bush focusing on the condition of women in Afghanistan, Iraq or Iran, when women still face violence and subjugation in the US.

Amalia: Indeed. We allow twelve-year-old and thirteen-year-old girls from Mexico, El Salvador, and Guatemala to come into the US and work in homes where they're essentially indentured servants. Their employers "invest" their money, so they only have enough to get back and forth, and when the time comes, they'll get their money back. So young girls of color who come here to work have absolutely no rights whatsoever. In fact, many of them are sexually abused in the households that they work in. At the same time, we're willing to develop *maquiladoras* along the Mexican border while taking no responsibility for what's happening in Juarez, where these mutilated, dismembered bodies of young girls have been found for years now. Hundreds and hundreds of girls and women have been killed, and nobody is talking about how American factories have legitimized their treatment, because no one is concerned about them once they leave their shift.

bell: Part of the racialized sexism wants everyone to think that a 15-year-old Mexican is not a girl, she's a woman. *We know she's a girl.* We can never emphasize this enough, because this is the fate of colored girls globally right now: the denial of their girlhood, the denial of their childhood, and the constant state of risk and danger they're living in. And in the US, the women working in these most vulnerable and underpaid positions, as caretakers of children, service workers, factory workers, are often young and Latina. But up until this spring, when hundreds of thousands of people took to the street in support of immigrant rights, they didn't have a public voice.

Amalia: Even going back to "nanny-gate," the focus was on the "servant problems" faced by the upper classes. No one acknowledged that these workers were primarily women, often Latina, and usually underpaid. Instead, the debate ended up being fuel for the anti-immigration fires.

The system I teach in, the California State University system, is beginning to utilize very unpleasant language around immigration and diversity, using terms like "tidal wave 1" and "tidal wave 2" and "post-tsunami" to describe demographic change. Obviously, these are not neutral terms—they refer to phenomena that inundates, overwhelms, and drowns. And despite the fact that there are many Asians in California, particularly in San Francisco, most of the time "immigrants" is a code word for Mexicans, and it sometimes refers to Central Americans.

It's unavoidable, and yet the language is the language of fear and deficit. It has nothing to do with "new resources" or "new opportunities," so correspondingly we're seeing an unwillingness to fund certain programs in public education. They don't want students who are remedial or students who might not speak English as their first language. To protect themselves from the "tidal waves," they set up policies and practices that prevent people from being educated—they build a wall.

bell: So we really have to go back to the extreme attack on bilingual education. Let's face it, even if you come to this country and you desperately want to learn English, if you have to work two or three jobs where you are completely in the background—like cleaning hotel rooms or working the back of restaurants—you're likely working on Saturdays and Sundays, and you're not presented with many chances to comfortably interact with others in English. When are you supposed to learn this new language?

Amalia: It's also about access. We insist that people learn English, but we don't offer English as a second language. The bulk of the immersion classes in public education are being filled by white students in Spanish classes whose parents have figured out that they need to be bilingual.

bell: Exactly.

Amalia: But at the same time, we are not offering enough classes in English as a second language for adults who are already here. They don't have the same opportunities to be bilingual.

One of the most radical things we've tried to do at our university is to give students credit for being native Spanish speakers. As a result, we have been able to move many of our students through language requirements by acknowledging that they already have mastered a second language that is viable and they don't have to learn French. If they're native Spanish speakers, they take an assessment and their language requirement is finished. We took a lot of heat for that, because people were saying knowing Spanish is not like knowing French, Italian, or German.

bell: This is a symptom of imperialist white supremacy, and other people of color, including African Americans, participate in the refusal to learn Spanish. I can't tell you how many schools I've visited where African American kids are being ushered into German and French. When I challenge people and say Spanish is the language to be learned, no one listens. The retort is, "Why would I learn Spanish? It's not the same class signifier as the others." Of course, it's tragic because many African Americans will be disenfranchised at work because they don't speak Spanish, which leads them to re-inscribe their racist attitudes that, "Mexicans are taking our jobs."

We see this, particularly in places like Miami, where many Black folks have not been able to move out of the working-class. They are in a rage against Spanish-speaking people who are finding jobs, but the fact that they're abused, demeaned or paid inadequately is not what's exposed. What fuels this racism on the part of Black people is that we live within a capitalist structure of diminishing returns. If you're struggling, you might not pick up on the fact that your tax dollars are subsidizing the military and the war, but you will get prompts to freak out about immigrants.

Amalia: The irony is poor Black people can be on the same side with white people about immigration. But I do think one of the dilemmas we constantly deal with is that race issues are largely articulated in Black and white terms.

I also think most Latinos have had an ahistorical education about Blacks in America, and most Blacks have had an ahistorical education about Mexicans in the southwest. Neither party is ready to understand how similar their struggles actually are, so when immigration comes up, we should be talking about human rights and civil rights, which could open a dialogue that Black people might want to enter. But because it's framed as a debate about language and nationality, not race and rights, some people support legislation that would prohibit immigrants from realizing their civil and human rights. Someday, this will come back to haunt them, because this legislation is based on the same principles which legalized racism.

bell: And I think we have to interrogate how the fate of Native Americans is included within that narrative, because the flip side of any narrative of immigration is a narrative about citizenship.

Amalia: Yes.

bell: Who has the right to be perceived as a citizen? In the current climate, this question has been reframed by the right. Now it's all about patriotic nationalism, and many people of color in the US feel silenced. They don't dare speak if they're poor, or if they're working in someone's home where they hear violent, abusive hate speech, but they can't resist because their resistance could be perceived as disloyal, unpatriotic, or in support of the "wrong people."

So much of the anti-immigration feeling carried by working-class Americans comes from the fear of losing citizenship rights and standing. For the millions of poor white people in the US, being perceived as "white" and as a "citizen" are their only badges of inclusion. If they're living in a tenement or a trailer with a bathroom that doesn't work and ten other people, they can still say they are citizens in a rich, democratic country, and they have the freedom to grow and self-actualize.

Amalia: And your only claim to status is feeling superior to the poorest brown worker who doesn't have papers, you don't have citizenship anyway! You know, all the work that was done on cultural citizenship was so radical, I'm not sure if it could be done now. These theorists described how people gain citizenship through the making of spaces, by creating identities and solidarities as workers, and by acting as cultural participants in society. Citizenship now is precisely what you're describing: loyalty to white supremacist thought and practice, with our belief in goodness residing somewhere between the flag, the fireman, and the soldier.

bell: And as a ten-year-old I knew the difference between citizenship and nationalism! I don't think we can talk about the average ten-year-old working-class kid in our nation understanding that distinction today.

Amalia: I would say that you could add ethnicity and language onto that paradigm where you're collapsing together citizenship and nationalism. It's more and more difficult for immigrants, even if they are here legally, to see themselves as citizens, because a citizen is a white English-speaking North American. So even when you gain those rights, you're not even sure that you can really exercise them.

One of the jokes among Chicanos is that a "Mexican" is just a "Chicano" waiting to happen. What will happen is that one or some of their rights will be breached, and as they become Chicanos, they will see that they can do something about it. Whereas, if they're still in the Mexican state, they might not feel empowered enough to take it on. Some people have asked me about the differences between Mexican Americans and Chicanos, and I say that defining yourself as a Chicano has to do with justice, agency, and the power to act on behalf of others. There is something about your earliest politicizing moments, when you exercise your right to dissent and fight.

With regards to divisions within the larger Latino community, one of the dilemmas we're facing now is how to create bridges between immigrant populations coming from Mexico and Central America who are largely indigenous and not Spanish-speaking. They might be learning English, but they've never mastered Spanish, so the connections between them and other Latinos are more tentative. So our activism has to evolve; we must make a space for people who are even different from us, and recognize the increasing complexity of what it means to be Latino in the US. This is something that the dominant culture doesn't understand, because they still think that anyone who comes from Latin America speaks Spanish.

bell: I mean, think about it—we're one of the few countries in the world without a grassroots movement for literacy. This is what allows many Americans to imagine that all Latin Americans speak Spanish; to conclude that everyone knows how to read and write English except for those "immigrants;" and to overlook how many American citizens are, in fact, remedial readers. That's why folks who can barely read are being even more disenfranchised, as so many of our interactions are computerized.

For example, there are so many barriers to travelling and getting around. For example, if you want to purchase an airline ticket, you have to pay a fee if you do it on the phone; if you do it on the Internet, you don't have to pay that fee. Well, I am an incredibly well-educated, well-renowned scholar, but I don't use the Internet. It's not a big deal for me to pay the fee; I can read and I can afford the difference. But what about all the people who are not fully literate, and who do not have computers in their homes? They're the ones who will be paralyzed. And when I think about all the different taxes and fees that have been instituted in the last few years, the impact on poor people is clear: it keeps people in their place, it keeps people confined, and it keeps people who don't have appropriate documents living in a state of absolute fear and dread.

Even those of us who have the right papers can be deemed by some higher authority, as I have been, as a "suspicious character." Now there's something in the computer that identifies me as "suspicious," and there's something that is put on my tickets which conveys this to people. I found this out because I asked why I was constantly searched at airports. What's frightening is that people don't want to acknowledge how many of the freedoms that defined us as different than more oppressive cultures are being taken away from us, because the romantic narrative of patriarchal nationalism has taken over. And I think it's important to note that we've seen a vicious resurgence of patriarchy, concurrent with the rise in militarism. This is having serious consequences, on issues ranging from housing to health care.

You know, we've talked about our bodies as the unidentified, invisible, work-me-to-death body, and we've also talked about the roles we play as caretakers. The other dimension we might want to touch on is the sick and diseased body of the person of color. Who cares for that body? Where is the medical system ready to recognize that body as worthy of optimal health care and optimal well-being? Many people in the US imagine that if people of color have money, we can enter the health care system and be treated as equals. As an upper-class Black woman, I know this is not the case. Money does not buy considerate care, and of course, the situation is much more grave for people without financial resources.

Black women die from breast cancer at a disproportionate rate, and the argument is that we don't go for care. Now, my mother has been going and they found a lump in her breast and the doctor she puts her trust in told her that her Medicare wouldn't pay for another mammogram for several months, "So why don't we just wait and see what happens with that lump?" And of course I say to my mother, "Mom, that's ridiculous. I've never heard of any doctor saying let's wait and see about that lump in your breast." But this is the kind of sexist, racist, and ageist health care which does not care about Black female and brown female bodies, nor for the elderly. I think the vast majority of health care discriminatory abuses occur with "unchaperoned" elderly patients, who are not accompanied by young people who may know, and ask, physicians the right questions.

Amalia: After my parents moved in with me, I had that role for about ten years. I accompanied them as often as I could to their doctors' appointments; I took notes; and I gave the doctor my card that says "Dr. Amalia Mesa-Bains" as soon as I arrived, because I wanted to make it clear to them that if they're going to treat my parents, they're going to have to be informed and they're going to have to share that knowledge. When they went by themselves, it wasn't always easy for them to understand the medical terminology, and it was really hard to get the information when they got back. So accompanying them on those visits became high priorities for me.

And having been through the medical system for the last couple of years as a result of a traumatic accident, I really understand that you can't get the best service unless you understand how the system works. I was lucky because I could go to people who were either wealthy or whose families had been in medicine, and I could say to them, if you were me and you had this problem, where would you go?

bell: Knowledge *is* power. For example, Black women in the US have had hysterectomies at a higher rate than women anywhere else in the Western world. But now hip and knee replacements have become the trendy surgeries to do on women of color, especially Black women, we who are the most obese women in this society. For all of her focus and attention to diet and weight, Oprah has never put a spotlight on these issues. If she were to put out a little book that spoke directly to Black women, working-class and poor women, and encourage us to deal with our health and preventable issues like diabetes, kidney failure, heart disease, it would be incredibly useful.

Amalia: Both of us have been on these journeys in the medical industrial complex, and we have been discovering how the health system works. One of the things I predict is that baby boomers are going to make demands on the health system; we're already insisting on being better informed, we're more engaged, and I think we're going to see changes because of that. Whether it's entitlement or privilege, as we hit the Medicare age in large numbers, we're going to pressure the existing system, so I don't think we know yet which way things are going to go.

bell: But I think that takes us back to the idea that health and housing are issues that broad coalitions can be built around. This is what I call practical activism—an activism that's connected to where you live, and to the vision of being homegrown. I believe that people of color, especially poor people of color, have deep concerns about living well, but they simply lack the resources to focus on health issues. Instead, day-to-day survival is paramount. And when we think about the impact of the war in Iraq on our lives, we know that there is going to be scarcity. We know that we'll be facing energy shortages. We already know that in many states welfare no longer pays for water, so we know there will be a time when individual people will not have access to water at certain times of the day. This is already happening, but because people of color have born the brunt of it, we have not had a public discourse about it.

Amalia: In California, on the central coast especially, there are big water conservation issues at play. For example, one of the reasons that our university cannot grow larger is that we don't have enough water credits to accomodate more people. So water is definitely being discussed here.

Another thing I've been thinking about is housing. There are some interesting models of creative housing, including those supported by the Center for Community Advocacy. They essentially help farm workers organize, start boycotts, and work with the people who own rundown, dilapidated and generally uninhabitable housing to upgrade it, so they can purchase it. So there are these models, but they're not in the big cities. They're in the smaller locations where people have to struggle so hard to even have a house to sleep in or an apartment, you know, where five or six families are rotating.

bell: This is definitely an issue in larger cities. For example, they've torn down so many projects in Chicago but they have not come up with affordable housing for poor people. The question that people ask about Chicago, Detroit, New York, and so on is where did those people go?

Amalia: San Francisco did it, too.

bell: So these people have gone into their cars, into the streets, and a lot of them have simply gone out of the cities because it's easier to be homeless elsewhere. It has become much more violent to be a homeless person in the city. You can drive through the hills of Kentucky and Virginia and see people living in cardboard boxes or shanty towns. And of course we both know that if you go to downtown L.A. after ten o'clock at night, you're going to see a world that looks like Brazil, that looks like any third world city, I mean, it's shocking. And Americans are not seeing that every night on their television screens.

You know, in many cities the state gives control over public housing to specific churches, and the churches get an economic kickback. It was initially presented as "community control," but many of them look like gated communities where the residents are tightly surveilled. Here, there is some evidence of an interlocking conservatism between church and state, which is something to keep our eyes on.

Amalia: This makes me think of the reach of the current Pope—this is the man that literally destroyed liberation theology in Latin America because his perspectives on Communism were informed by a Cold War context, and he couldn't understand that social justice and advocacy within the church could actually be productive in Latin America. That coupled the Church's deepening retrogression regarding women in the church, as well as homophobia, are the mark of this man.

bell: His rise also coincides tragically with the passing of voices who brought us the vision of education as the practice of freedom and of liberation theology. I think of people like Essex Hemphill, Marlin Riggs, June Jordan, Gloria Anzaldúa. These radical people of color were, in some ways, at the forefront of new discourses.

Amalia: When you lose people like this, you lose their iconic power, and their productive years—what they could have thought, written, or said with more time. We started a project called "Regeneration" about ten years ago primarily because we didn't want to be dinosaurs; we didn't want to be the last of our kind. Others had to be willing to see art not simply as commerical goods, but as a space of resistance and affirmation.

bell: We have to continue to cultivate young people who will be willing to critique greed, because one of the forces that has been incredibly deradicalizing has been the longing for wealth. I think this cuts across race and class in the US; even many young radicals long for wealth if they don't come from it. So we have to nurture a culture of compassion and generosity that is critical of imperialist capitalism.

Amalia: One of the things that has always been a hallmark of the artist, writer, and cultural worker in the Chicano community is service to the community. Your gifts and talents, your abilities, your treasures are only valuable if they are going to go back, in some way, to your community, to your family. But "professional-ization" has crept into our community organizations. Now, "you're on your way" only if "somewhere" is out of your community.

bell: Many young people are motivated by wealth or ce-lebrity. Take the lottery. It symbolizes unearned wealth, and the idea that you can be lucky. It trades on the magical notion that wealth can just come out of the blue. And some people can't get their minds off of it. It's one way we collude with the mythologies of imperialist capitalism, because of those myths that tell you that wealth will heal you and your life.

Amalia: So we're back to health, back to what heals you.

bell: Yes. And what we hope to offer readers with these conversations are multiple visions of wholeness.

Amalia: Somehow in this process of these multiple con-versations, you and I have been exchanging our lives as they have been lived in moments of extremity. And the discussions that have surfaced here are certainly connected to the exterior lives we have led as recognized and powerful women of color—in your case, you are known nationally and internationally. But our exterior lives are only a part of this dialogue. During this exchange, you and I lived through moments of extremity, and we often had to rely on our interior lives to find the balance to survive, to be as whole as we could be. These conversations reflect this process as well.

bell: I think about people like Toni Cade Bambara and June Jordan, who were rare among African American women thinkers and cultural workers, because they always spoke to "regular Black folks," not just academics nor committed activists. This was their constituency in the US, and internationally, yet we see how quickly they can be forgotten. Even when Andrea Dworkin died at 58, one of the most militant, dissident voices within American feminism, so many people I spoke with didn't know who she was. Already too many people have forgotten Audre Lorde.

So I think that it's important for us to recognize that our conversation has another value: it helps us protect and preserve our legacies. You know, part of my longing to do a conversation book with you kicked in when we first met. You were a brilliant, creative woman, surviving happily, and because you are ten years older than me, I knew that some of how you have made your way in this world was a light unto my path. I knew I could learn from you, and when you and I talk about grassroots coalition building, we are often talking about dialogues between women.

Amalia: Between women, over kitchen tables just like this one.

bell: Over kitchen tables and daycare centers, in shelters—because a lot of consciousness-raising around domestic violence takes place in shelters—and within the prison system. I think our conversation is especially meaningful, because it publicly represents the value and meaning of dialogue across boundaries.

We also recognize the deep and profound grief we feel because we will not be able to dialogue with Toni Cade Bambara,

Gloria Anzaldúa, June Jordan, or any of the many other visionary thinkers who have passed away too soon. In some ways, it is
an indictment of our intellectual laziness that we have not always
made the time to document our shared work and thinking.

For you and I, this has been an effort: we live on different
coasts, we're struggling with different health issues. But we have
made the time for this conversation, and now we have this record
of our triumph. *homegrown* documents the ability of a Chicana and
an African American woman to meet one another, speak through
our differences, and find our commonalities.

ABOUT THE AUTHORS

Amalia Mesa-Bains is a California-based artist, curator and writer who has been associated with a number of pioneering exhibitions of Latino art, including *Chicano Art: Resistance and Affirmation* and *Mi Alma, Mi Tierra, Mi Gente: Contemporary Chicana Art*. Her powerful work incorporates various aspects of Chicano culture and folk traditions, and explores religion and ritual, Chicana history, female rites of passage, and the role each plays in the development of the Latina psyche. Mesa-Bains won the MacArthur "Genius" Award in 1992, and is the Director of Visual and Public Art at California State University, Monterey Bay.

bell hooks has been called one of the leading public intellectuals of her generation. She has written extensively and persuasively on the emotional impact of racism and sexism, as well as the importance of political engagement with art and the media. In her recent work on love, relationships, and community, she shows how emotional health is a necessary component to effective resistance and activism. Her books include *Ain't I A Woman: Black Women and Feminism*; *All About Love: New Visions*; *Black Looks: Race and Representation*; *Breaking Bread: Insurgent Black Intellectual Life* (with Cornel West); *Communion: The Female Search for Love*; *Feminism is for Everybody: Passionate Politics*; *Feminist Theory: From Margin to Center*; and *Teaching to Transgress: Education and the Practice of Freedom*.

ABOUT SOUTH END PRESS

South End Press is an independent, collectively run book publisher with more than 250 titles in print. Since our founding in 1977, we have met the needs of readers who are exploring, or are already committed to, the politics of radical social change. We publish books that encourage critical thinking and constructive action on the key political, cultural, social, economic, and ecological issues shaping life in the United States and in the world. South End Press provides a forum for a wide variety of democratic social movements and an alternative to the products of corporate publishing.

From its inception, South End has organized itself as an egalitarian collective with decision-making arranged to share as equally as possible the rewards and stresses of running the business. Each collective member is responsible for core editorial and administrative tasks, and all collective members earn the same base salary. South End also has made a practice of inverting the pervasive racial and gender hierarchies in traditional publishing houses; our collective has been majority women since the mid-1980s, and at least 50 percent people of color since the mid-1990s. Our author list—which includes bell hooks, Arundhati Roy, Noam Chomsky, Winona LaDuke, Manning Marable, Ward Churchill, Cherríe Moraga, and Howard Zinn—reflects South End's commitment to publish on myriad issues from diverse perspectives.

To expand access to information and critical analysis, South End Press has been instrumental to the start of two on-going political media projects—Speak Out and *Z Magazine*. We have worked closely with a number of important media and research institutions including Alternative Radio, Political Research Associates, and the Committee on Women, Population, and the Environment.